PIERRE LEPROHON

Michelangelo Antonioni:

AN INTRODUCTION

TRANSLATED BY SCOTT SULLIVAN

SIMON AND SCHUSTER, NEW YORK, 1963

Contents

Acknowledgments

For their collaboration in this work, the author wishes to thank
Dominique Blanchar, Alba de Cespedes and Rina Macrelli; Alain
Cuny, Giovanni Fusco and Jean-Pierre Mocky. Our thanks also
go to Guido Aristarco, Jacques Doniol-Valcroze, Dominique Fernandez, Alberto Moravia and Tino Ranieri, who have given us
kind permission to reproduce selections from their critical writings; also to the publishing houses Einaudi and Guanda for the
sections by Italo Calvino and Fabio Carpi, and to the newspapers
and magazines which have permitted us to reprint various articles
by, or quotations from, Antonioni. Finally, and especially, we
thank Signor Antonioni himself, who has closely followed and
supported our work.

We should like to thank the following firms and individuals for
their help in supplying illustrations for this book: Gamma-Film;
Marceau-Cocinor; Athos-Films; C.C.F.C.; Artistes Associés; Rina
Macrelli and Pierre Kalfan.

The American publishers of this volume also wish to thank
Jonas Mekas, editor of *Film Culture*, for his kind assistance on
numerous occasions; Cyrus Harvey, Jr., of Janus Films; Blowitz,
Thomas and Canton, Inc., Lopert Pictures Corp., Astor Pictures,
Inc., and Gideon Bachmann, for providing illustrations; the various
magazines which gave permission for the reprinting of articles.

Editor's Note: We have in this volume referred to each of Antonioni's films by its original Italian title except when quoting from a
published source where an English title was used.

I

MICHELANGELO ANTONIONI:

THE MAN AND HIS WORK

•

1. Early Life and the Documentaries

With the popular and critical success of *L'Avventura,* Michelangelo Antonioni achieved the position he always deserved. He now stands in the forefront of the cinema of the future: a cinema from which only the future will be able to tell us what to expect. He is one of the outstanding directors in the world today, both because of the innovations he has brought to his art—making concrete and orderly what had in other hands been no more than confused, wavering aspirations—and because of the beautiful quality of his work.

Long unappreciated, if not unknown, attacked, misunderstood or neglected by numerous critics, Antonioni had to wait ten years for people to be aware that his work has an entirely new ring. Today we can also appreciate the internal unity of his whole production, a production which, although limited in the number of films comprising it, includes practically no waste and is marked from beginning to end by an entirely personal style and set of themes.

André Gide once wrote a sentence which might be applied with great accuracy to Antonioni's work: "He carries within himself what is needed to disorient and to surprise, that is to say, what is needed to endure."

Antonioni has disoriented and surprised many critics. They failed to recognize the true, revolutionary character of his films because it was veiled by a discreetness of expression, a quiet formalism. In the face of this widespread incomprehension, Antonioni did not become discouraged, nor has he tried to "explain" himself. He has continued in his own direction. "One does not work for the public," he wrote in 1958, "but the public is there all the same, and they are the ones who are watching. I know very well that I ought

11

to push myself to make less difficult films, but I am afraid that I might lose my sincerity. Perhaps I shall get to that point spontaneously."

To understand the importance of Antonioni's work, we must glance back over the history of the motion picture. During the first thirty years, it strained to become an autonomous art form. With the addition of the spoken word, it became a different form which was purified and rationalized over the next thirty years. In its latest stage, it suffered a hardening of the arteries. It took Antonioni to make clear the necessity for a further renovation, which had already been bubbling in the creative crucible for several years.

We are now witnessing the emergence of something far more important than "new techniques"—of a cinema of behavior, which is renewing the art in its content and hence also in its form. I shall not enlarge at this point on the horizons opened up by this third major step in the development of the cinema, on the liberating effect it promises to have, on the stereotypes it is likely to create nor on the limitations it imposes upon an art which may perhaps be destined to fulfill quite different purposes. But one fact is undeniable. While the "New Wave" floundered, fighting battles which were no more than rear-guard actions, Antonioni's work was there all along to emphasize the vanity of such pointless agitation. Since *Le Amiche, Il Grido,* and *L'Avventura,* the revolution has been in effect. A new kind of cinema exists.

Antonioni lives today in an apartment in a residential section of Rome. The office in which he works—with books everywhere, a scattering of abstract paintings—overlooks the roofs and terraces of Rome. There he has remained, very much himself, faithful to his early hopes, in a profession which changes so many men and shatters so many ideals.

Michelangelo Antonioni was born in Ferrara, on the border between Emilia and Venezia, on September 29, 1912. He is a man of the north—calm, reserved, demanding; with a sharp profile, a steady eye, the silhouette of an aristocrat, and a character as complex as his films. He stands as far from Rossellini's fiery enthusiasms as he does from Fellini's dreamy nonchalance; he measures his words and never gives himself away. The seriousness with which he treats everything he deals with, the gravity of his speech, all contrast with the usual image we have of his countrymen. But his external calm hides an extreme sensitivity and a nervousness which is occasionally betrayed by a tic that plays across his face. His character is a collection of contrasts: "A modest man of passion, a classical lyricist," as one critic has written. Tall, thin, pale, with a sad smile, a friendly glance.

His childhood and early youth were spent in Ferrara, "a marvelous little city on the Paduan plain, antique and silent."[1] When he was about ten years old, Michelangelo Antonioni began to design puppets and stick figures, but not in the way most children do. He sketched architectural settings for them, with portals and columns, then daubed these very precise drawings with spots of violent color. He also amused himself by building towns of cardboard or wood, or from his Erector set, and then filling them with little people about whom he made up stories.

"Houses interested me; not only the exteriors but the interiors as well. Often I would climb up to a window to see who and what were inside."[2]

From the age of fourteen to eighteen, Antonioni painted in oils, mostly portraits. This taste for architecture and painting has not left him. He still produces a canvas from time to time, and in his films he often has an architect among the characters. He is able to elicit psychological as well as plastic expression from an architectural setting, as in *L'Avventura*, with the baroque complexes at Noto, or in *La Notte*, with the modern architecture of Milan.

He once said, however, in a seminar with students at the Experimental Film Center in Rome: "The experience which has been most important in making me the director I have become is that of the middle-class background from which I come and in which I was brought up. It was that world which contributed most to my predilection for certain themes, certain problems, certain emotional and psychological conflicts."[3] Although Antonioni's boyhood in Ferrara was rather peaceful, the games he played brought him into contact with children of a lower social station than his own. He experienced feelings of shame about his better education, his more expensive clothing.

He went to the University of Bologna for his advanced studies but continued to live in Ferrara, commuting the twenty-five miles' distance by train every day. "I began in the liberal arts, but I fell in love with a girl who was at the Technical Institute, so I transferred there." On graduating from the Institute, he enrolled in courses in economics and business. "I made an effort to learn some of the concepts involved in higher mathematics, which are now very useful to me." Antonioni eventually received his diploma from the University of Bologna as *dottore* in economics and business.

Meanwhile, the taste for the plastic arts which he had demonstrated in his early youth was to branch off toward the theater. Antonioni wrote three or four plays; then, with a few other students, he formed a student company. It included Giorgio Bassani and Lanfranco Caretti, both of whom were later to achieve fame —the first as a writer, the second as a philologist. In Ferrara, these young people put on their own plays, and those of other authors such as Pirandello and Ibsen, including one by Antonioni ("Terrible!" he has said of it), with Antonioni as director.

At the same time, he was publishing his first stories, or "prose poems," as they were called in the local newspaper *Il Corriere Padano*.[4] Soon after, he began to write film criticism. The cinema was, along with tennis (at which he won a number of tournaments), the young student's main distraction. "I went very often, and almost always alone." His film criticism in *Il Corriere Padano* was extremely severe and soon earned him the hatred of the owners of the local film houses, as well as considerable difficulty with the paper's editors. By attacking the Italian films of the period he was implicitly attacking the Fascist regime which produced them, and as a result, his articles were often cut and mutilated.

It was at about this period that Antonioni first experimented with film-making himself; he tells the story in the following words:

"The first time I ever looked through a camera (a Bell and Howell 16 mm.) was in a lunatic asylum. . . . I had got the idea into my head that I wanted to shoot a documentary directly from life, in other words, with real patients, and I was so insistent that finally the director of the asylum said to me, 'Let's try it.'

"We set up the camera and the lights; the madmen were arranged around the room according to the requirements of the first scene. They obeyed our instructions humbly and paid very close attention in order to avoid making mistakes. Their behavior was touching, and I was pleased to see how things were working out. Finally I ordered the lights to be turned on. I was a little nervous. All at once the room was filled with blinding light. For an instant, the patients remained motionless, as if petrified. Never have I seen on the face of any actor such an expression of terror. This lasted only a moment, and then an indescribable scene took place. The madmen sought desperately for shelter from the light, as if it were some sort of prehistoric monster attacking them, and their faces—which before had been calm—became convulsed and devastated. And then it was our turn to be petrified. The camera-man did not even have the strength to stop his machine, nor was I capable of giving any orders whatever. It was the director of the asylum who finally cried, 'Stop! Lights out!' And in the half-darkened room, we could see a swarm of bodies twisting as if in the last throes of a death agony."[5]

This experiment was to remain the only one of its kind, but it reveals what attracted Antonioni to the cinema: its value as psychological documentation, that interior realism which he was later to search for and to find, beyond the limits of Italian neorealism.

As a critic, Antonioni's literary style—judging by a few extracts from the prose poems of this period—was rather close to the "precious": the "calligraphy" that Lattuada and Castellani were soon to introduce to the Italian cinema in an attempt to avoid the swaggering Fascist style.

In these aesthetic trial runs of his youth one can already see rising to the surface Antonioni's passion for man, in terms of what makes him act, what he feels, as distinguished from his social status—or because of it. Here is the way he paints the portrait of a peasant he glimpsed on returning from a trip to the mountains: "He was like a piece of that earth, the earth he cultivated every day, indefatigably; a sun-baked piece, somewhat resembling us as we returned from the snowfields, but to a higher degree, cooked to a further point, more durable; he was spotted, burned, and he drank, he drank. . . .

"I really did not know whether the truth lay with us who were returning, our baggage laden with the memory of variegated pleasures, brilliant hotels—or with them, emerging from the night, rich only with their own fatigue; whether it lay in our existence, marked with the blemish of perpetual dissatisfaction, tormented by the impossibility of ever achieving satiety—or in theirs, where thoughts, instincts and desires are mingled in one single, crude thought, so easily appeased. . . ."[6]

"The blemish of perpetual dissatisfaction . . ." Already Antonioni, ill at ease with his middle-class background but not yet fully conscious of his vocation, was setting down the theme of the major works that he was to produce twenty years later.

At the end of 1939, having decided to try to make his career in the cinema, he realized that he would have to leave Ferrara for Rome. His whole youth had slipped away in this northern land where the winter is long and the days often gray and glowering. This, too, was to leave its imprint on his work; this setting and atmosphere were to pervade all his films, even when he transported the action to a southern locale.

But in Rome he had to live. "I took the offer of a job at the World's Fair.[7] I kept it only a few months. I made a lot of money at that job, but I could not stand the idea of wasting time doing work that absorbed me without giving me anything in return. So I handed in my resignation and took a job as an editor on the magazine *Cinema.*"

At that time, *Cinema* was officially called "the organ of the Fascist Entertainment Guild" and its official director was none less than Mussolini's son, Vittorio. "Sheltered behind this prestigious puppet, two young editors of *Cinema*, Gianni Puccini and Domenico Purificato, were able to lead the magazine in an anti-Fascist direction, with the complicity of Francesco Pasinetti, the professor of cinema history at the Experimental Film Center."[8] At the Luce Institute, also, workers in the film industry were quietly preparing for a revolt against the Fascist style. From this fermentation, neorealism was to be born, which was both an expression of political opinion and an aesthetic concept.[9] The movement was reinforced as more and more young men joined after 1940: Giuseppe de Santis, Mario Alicato, Guido Aristarco, Carlo Lizzani, Glauco Viazzi, Ugo Casiraghi—and Michelangelo Antonioni.

Antonioni published his first articles in *Cinema* at the beginning of 1940. He continued to contribute for several months, but had frequent run-ins with Rosario Leone, the secretary of Vittorio Mussolini. Antonioni was finally fired, ostensibly because of an editorial mistake, but actually for political reasons.

He then found himself in Rome without a job. "None of those whom I had considered my friends offered a helping hand. I spent several months really alone. I did not want to run to my father for aid because he would certainly have asked me to return to Ferrara where several jobs had been offered me, some of them quite impressive, but jobs as someone else's employee, which did not interest me. Thus I had to work out my problems on my own. Rome is a hard and hostile town. I spent months in hell, really suffering from hunger. One day I even stole a steak. . . ."

During this difficult period Antonioni did not forget his real goal. He enrolled in the Experimental Film Center, but spent only three months there. "The technical side of films, by and for itself, has never interested me. Once one has learned the two or three basic rules of cinematographic grammar, he can do what he likes, including breaking those rules."

While at the Center, he made a short documentary which won him a first prize. This little film (there was just over 250 feet of it) consisted apparently of only one continuous scene. A woman is shown paying a visit to another woman after a blackmailing incident; she is trying to recover certain compromising letters. The camera concentrates on the first woman from the beginning and then, with a panning shot, reveals the second. Actually, the pan consisted of two separate shots spliced together, and both roles were played by the same actress, but no one was able to discover at what point the splice had been made.

Antonioni describes his career after he left the Experimental Center as follows:

"My first professional activity consisted in putting together a scenario that one of my acquaintances had asked me to write for him. I was promised two thousand lire for the job; I believe I got half that much. I wrote the scenario from the first to the last line without having the slightest idea of how such work was done. The film was never made, for other reasons. My second job was with Rossellini, writing the scenario for *Un Pilota Ritorna* with him and several others. Rossellini had moved to Rome only shortly before this time. He lived in an almost empty house; there was a large bed in one room, a table and a few chairs in another, the rest was empty. Roberto was nearly always in bed. We worked there, on the bed. Later I was introduced to some people at Scalera [Scalera Films, a major production company], toward the end of 1942. There I worked on the scenario of *I Due Foscari.*[10] At this time, we saw a good deal of Enrico Fulchignoni, a theatrical director who had had considerable success, particularly in directing Thornton Wilder's *Our Town.* I did what I could to insure that the direction of the film was assigned to him.

"Meanwhile, I had been drafted. A hellish period began in my life. I used to escape from the army camp every night in order to work on the film, and return at dawn. I was completely stupefied with fatigue. It was a very cold winter; I still have the image in my mind's eye of that camp in the livid dawn. I had to scale a wet, icy wall, or crawl through the mud under a hedge, to return to camp without being seen.

"When the shooting began I managed to get leave. The cameraman on the film was Ubaldo Arata, a man of whom I still have very fond memories. He was an excellent cameraman, but, like all the Italians of that period, he worked empirically, without any technical training at all. We got on very well. During the course of the shooting, I made some personal experiments. For example, I discovered that when a wide-angle lens (a 25, for instance) is used to film a scene in a room, the actors should walk with shorter steps. Otherwise, the room, made to appear very long by such a lens, could be covered in a very few steps. Everyone was afraid of using white at that time. The walls of houses were pink; shirts and tablecloths were pink or yellow. I succeeded in persuading Arata to shoot white objects as well. The effect was surprising for the period and for the type of film we were using.

"Arata became very friendly toward me and spoke of me in the best of terms, so it seems, to Scalera [Michele Scalera, head of Scalera Films]. One day, the latter called me to his office and said

to me, 'Do you want to go to France to work with Carné?' Carné
was one of the greatest directors of the day, and I was overjoyed.
But I still had my military obligations. How could I go abroad
when I was suposed to be in the army? I did incredible things; I
had half of Rome working at it, and in the end, I managed to get
special leave. I left, hoping to find some way of getting across
the border without a visa when I reached Mentone. I had to stay
at Mentone for about twenty days. The town was sad and deserted, and I was eating my heart out with impatience. Finally the
visa arrived. I took the train and went to Paris. It was a Sunday.
Carné was working at the Joinville-le-Pont studios in the suburbs
of Paris. He made me wait more than a half hour before he saw
me. For me, he was at that time the great Carné, and I was very
moved when I found myself face to face with him. I explained to
him who I was, and said that Scalera had sent me as assistant director for the Italian part of the film that he was then shooting,
Les Visiteurs du Soir. Carné looked me over with unconcealed
ill will. Then he said, 'Well, my friend, you've got eyes. Look.' And
after that, he did not say another word to me.[11] Some time later
we went to Nice for the exterior shots. I remember that I traveled
almost the whole way on the steps of the railway carriage. I had
not been able to get inside because it was so crowded. Some of
my comrades were in the same situation, but I was in the worst
spot of all. It was then that Carné spoke to me for the second
time. Obviously he was concerned about the possibility of an accident for which he might be held at least partly responsible. I
stayed with Carné till the end of the film, that is, several months.
In Nice, I lived at the Hotel Negresco, where I became acquainted
with the nursemaid of a rich family and got the idea of making a
film on the backstage life of a great hotel. I spent my time in the
hidden corners of that hotel, making many notes. Later I lost the
notebook.

"During the shooting of *Les Visiteurs du Soir,* I made friends
with Alain Cuny[12] and with Aldo[13], who was the film's photographer. The script girl, Mme Witta, was also kind to me. Carné, on
the other hand, continued to treat me very badly. There was one
thing that I always kept hidden from him: the fact that I had
come to France with a contract from Scalera to be co-director of

the film, and not assistant director. I took great care not to bring this up. So great was the admiration I had for him that it seemed to me absurd to introduce myself as his co-director. Carné didn't understand my political position at that time; I was much more on his side, on the French side, than he probably imagined, and I was as ashamed as if I had been a thief, to be a compatriot of those who had occupied the South of France.

"I also met Prévert.

"I ought to have stayed on in France and worked with Grémillon and Cocteau. (This, at least, is what they told me at Scalera). But my leave had run out in the meantime, and I had to return to Rome in haste."

But Michelangelo Antonioni was not ready to give up his ambition to direct a film himself. He had succeeded in obtaining the Luce Institute's backing to make a documentary about the fishermen and riverbank dwellers of the lower Po valley. Thus he returned to Ferrara to make his first financed film, a film which, in its theme, its style, its setting and even its difficulties, prefigures everything that the director was later to produce.

The shooting lasted a month, at the end of which time Antonioni brought back to Rome footage which would have been ample for the two-reel film he had originally planned.

"I ought to say one thing, even at the risk of appearing presumptuous. While I was shooting my first documentary, Visconti was shooting *Ossessione. Gente del Po* was a documentary on river life, fishermen: on *men*, that is, not on things or places. I was, without knowing it, following the same path as Visconti. I remember very well how much I regretted not being able to give my subject matter a narrative development or to turn it into a film with a 'theme.' Today, perhaps, I would be cited in a discussion of the birth of neorealism. Thus it seems to me that, rather than speak of a documentary influence in my feature films, it would be more accurate to speak of the narrative tendency in my documentaries."[14]

A series of crucial events overwhelmed Italy at this time. On July 24, 1943, Mussolini was forced to resign and was put under arrest. An armistice was signed with the Allies on November 9, but the Germans occupied the country, while the Allies landed in Campania on the following day. On November 12, Mussolini, who had been liberated by a Nazi commando group, proclaimed the creation of a new Fascist regime, the so-called Republic of Salo.

"The period of the German occupation was very hard. Film-making in Rome came to a halt. I began to do translations as the only means of earning a little money. I translated Morand's *Monsieur Zéro*, Gide's *La Porte Étroite* and Chateaubriand's *Atala*. But it became dangerous for me to remain in Rome; I had begun to be involved in underground activity with my friends in the Action Party, and twice I barely missed being arrested by the Germans with copies of the newspaper *Italia Libera* in my pocket. I went to Abruzzi, a region which had not yet been occupied, but after a few weeks the Germans arrived there, too. I had to flee, this time to a country cottage. One morning we were awakened by violent knocking on the door; it was the Germans once again. They were looking for a hidden radio set. Fortunately they did not arrest us. Finally I returned to Rome, where I was able to live by selling the cups and medals I had won in tennis tournaments.

"Like everyone who worked in films, I had received highly attractive offers from the new party [the Mussolini regime] to go north. I knew that my mother was ill and I would have liked to be nearer to her. But my revulsion against Fascism was too strong and I stayed in Rome. Italy was divided into two parts. There was no longer any communication between them. At the end of the war I learned that my mother had died a year before."

Antonioni went back to his translations and adaptations. He was film critic for *Italia Libera;* Rome had been liberated in 1944 and the newspaper was now being published openly. He also wrote for most of the journals in which the precursors of neorealism and the young critics from *Cinema,* (which had suspended publication) were at last able to express their views freely, tolling the death knell of the "white telephone style" and "calligraphy." We find Antonioni's byline in *Film d'Oggi, Film Rivista* and again in *Cinema,* when it resumed publication in 1947.

After the war ended, Antonioni plunged into film work to make up for lost time. Between 1946 and 1948, he collaborated in the writing of several scenarios. One was an adaptation of Giuseppe de Santis' *Caccia Tragica;* he also participated in its filming in the north of Italy. Two other scenarios entitled *Furore* and *The Trial of Maria Tarnowska* were written in collaboration with Visconti. Neither was ever produced. The first was the story of an all-girl orchestra that went to play at the front. If this film had been made, it would have been the first Italian picture on the war and the occupation, and it might have taken the place of *Open City.* The second treated a sensational trial which had been held in Venice in 1911. It was the story of a Russian woman and her life in a rich, corrupt society—a setting which Visconti might have been able to portray most effectively. Work on the scenario took six months; then the whole project fell through. Antonioni retired to Merano to recover from nervous exhaustion.

During the war, the reels of his documentary *Gente del Po* had been sent to Venice. After the liberation of that city, Antonioni set out in search of his film. He found part of it in a warehouse; another part proved to be unusable when developed; and all the sequences that had been shot in the delta village—the most tragic part of the entire film—were missing. Antonioni is convinced that they were deliberately destroyed. In 1947, what remained of *Gente del Po*—only a thousand out of two thousand feet—was edited and distributed. Its appearance enabled Antonioni to return to directing. Between 1948 and 1950 he made several more short films (a list of these may be found in the back of this book). They deal with a wide range of subjects, from the rayon industry and a funicular railway to labor conditions and peasant magic. They include a critical work on the "True Confessions" department of the popular press—from which emerged the idea that bloomed four years later as *Lo Sceicco Bianco* ("The White Sheik"), written by Antonioni with Fellini and Pinelli. In every case, the director's interest was focused on the human beings involved: the Roman street sweepers in the empty hours just before dawn; peasants deeply attached to their traditions; the pitiful stars of the photographic comic strips and the poor idiots who read them. The funicular railway at Cortina d'Ampezzo served him as a pretext for expressing the feeling of dizziness, which he took pains to experience first himself. And everywhere we feel, piercing through to the surface, "his pessimism, his incurable feel-

Gente del Po

ing of solitude," as the Italian critic Fabio Carpi has phrased it.

The photography in these short films—particularly in *Gente del Po* and *Netteza Urbana*—has the special characteristics that are to be found in his feature films. Also, the musical scores mark the beginning of Antonioni's collaboration with Giovanni Fusco (see page 165). In *Netteza Urbana*, Antonioni wanted to have a saxophone arrangement of a Bach prelude to complement the jazz arrangements written by Fusco, but a musicographer from Lux Films (the producer) cried sacrilege and it was played on the piano.

Antonioni's documentaries are too often neglected by critics. They contain the seeds of his major works, and are sometimes freer experiments than the full-length films that followed. In *Gente del Po*, the tragic depiction of the people's misery was as revolutionary a force in the documentary field as *Ossessione* in the narrative; as unusual a work in contrast with Emmer's and Gras's art films as was *Ossessione* in contrast with *Tosca* and *Scipio Africanus*.

2. The First Features: *Cronaca di un Amore, I Vinti, La Signora senza Camelie*

Antonioni returned to Rome from Cortina d'Ampezzo to try to get backing for a full-length film of his own. "In 1950 I found a man from Turin who was willing to finance a film for me. I proposed the theme of *Cronaca di un Amore*, but he did not like it. I insisted, and he finally said, 'Come see me. If you can convince me, we'll make the film.'

"I went to see him. He lived in a hotel. In that hotel room, I talked steadily for four or five hours; anyone who knows me will understand how difficult this was for me. I had an unknown face opposite me. I did not know how to talk, since I had always preferred to remain silent. My words brought expressions to his face which were incomprehensible to me. At last he told me that he still didn't like the subject, but he understood that I liked it very much, and that was enough for him."[1]

The action of the film is set in Milan, in the grayness of the Lombard winter, in an industrial suburb echoing with the roar of passing trains. Antonioni went to Milan to shoot it, thus beginning his first big picture at the age of thirty-eight with no more technical training than his three months at the Experimental Center and what he had taught himself while making his documentaries. But he already knew precisely what he wanted to achieve. He immediately adopted a revolutionary technique, of which people took notice at the time, although few realized exactly what it promised for the future.

"My habit of shooting rather long scenes was born spontaneously on the first day of filming *Cronaca di un Amore*. Having the camera fixed to its stand immediately caused me real discomfort. I felt paralyzed, as if I were being prevented from following closely the one thing in the film that interested me: I mean, the characters. The next day, I called for a dolly, and I began to follow my characters till I felt the need to move on to another exercise. For me, this was the best way to be real, to be true. Real: inside the scene, exactly as in life. I have never succeeded in composing a scene without having the camera with me, nor have I ever been able to make my characters talk in accordance with a pre-established script, or to follow the development laid down by such a script. Already, even then, I needed to *see* the characters, to see even their simplest gestures, after everything had been said, after the last speech had been spoken, when nothing more remained but the consequences of what had occurred in each person's soul. My technique came into being as a function of two things: the camera and the actors."[2]

We shall see a little later how this technique was to become, in Pierre Billard's phrase, "the ABC of the young modern cinema."

The scenario offers less obvious novelty. It turns on an act of adultery and its fatal consequences, somewhat as in James Cain's novel, *The Postman Always Rings Twice* (which has been adapted for the screen several times, *Ossessione* being one Italian version). The couple has committed a criminal act in their own minds; they have been saved by luck from murder, and they know perfectly well that they are guilty. Fate has simply outdistanced them. The husband's death ruins their love and separates them forever.

It is easy to see in this film "a transalpine version of the American crime films of the Forties. . . . Criminal lovers, suspicious husband, private detectives, hotel rooms, fast cars, as well as more ordinary everyday elements of modern life, all show up at their appointed time."[3] Antonioni appears to be using a certain crime-fiction formula, a familiar dramatic concept, and to be accepting a commonplaceness of props and accessories. But he uses it in such a way that although there is drama—feelings of guilt, violent passions—the film is basically antidramatic. Events are only appearances; reality lies within the characters. Because it is that reality alone which interests the director, it is on them alone—the characters—that he expends his interest. As he was to do later and even more boldly in *L'Avventura,* Antonioni here conjures up the barest details of a plot, the only purpose of which is to set the characters' passions in motion. We shall never know whether or not the couple did away with the man's fiancée, whether the husband was the victim of an accident or committed suicide, whether or not the woman and her lover will be indicted at the inquest. In just the same way, we shall never know what became of Anna on the mysterious island. But we do know that their passion has been shattered, that they have been irrevocably parted. *Cronaca di un Amore* leaves its central characters in the emptiness of a passion which has devoured itself. In theme and technique (which we shall discuss below), it throws much light on the internal unity of Antonioni's work.

Not all critics have granted it such an important position. François Truffaut wrote in 1954: "What insincerity, what phoniness, what a disappointment."[4] And it is clear that *Cronaca di un Amore* suffers from certain influences, both French and American. But in the end, the work departs from these influences. When the film first opened in Paris in 1951, one French critic saw into the director's future when he emphasized the ways in which Antonioni had refused to accept a dramatic theme or bow to dramatic requirements. He wrote: "The story develops with the rhythm of its own purely internal necessity. In its unfolding, which owes nothing at all to the rules of the drama, it spins no plot; on the contrary, it draws out a discursive tale to which the word 'End' is written only after the play of events has dispersed its three characters."[5]

The fact that the film was made at the height of neorealism is no less significant. The Italian films of 1950 were beginning to move away from the facts of the war itself, to deal with its consequences, plunging into the heart of a population torn with misery and unemployment and forced into surrendering every principle. Antonioni was the first to apply neorealistic concepts in a middle-class setting without at the same time returning to past techniques. He enlarged the new school's domain, led it to seek the truth at new social levels, while simultaneously guiding his own dramatic testimony in an introspective direction. In a certain sense, he also renovated its style, and it is understandable that André Bazin should have written that *Cronaca di un Amore* was "something like the *Dames du Bois de Boulogne* of neorealism."

With this first film, Antonioni succeeded in fixing the quality which was to form the principal merit of all his works, a kind of magic, produced by both the beauty of the images and the effectiveness of the rhythm binding them together. Long scenes (which represented a significant advance in technique) alternate with elliptical editing, all tending to leave the smallest possible space to actual events and bringing the full violence of the scenes to bear on the characters' feelings, on their instincts. The luxurious interiors and the elegant costumes of the star, Lucia Bose, contrast with the sordid exteriors and the rainy, nocturnal atmosphere of the Milanese suburb. These contrasts are expressed in the very predicaments of the characters; they set the lovers in opposition to each other, tied together though they are by their carnal passion, as though they suffered from a curse that could be exorcised only by a crime—contemplated or committed. The elegance of the writing and the beauty of the acting add to the cruelty of the theme. In place of the conventional film's "explanations," Antonioni has already begun to substitute the attitudes and behavior of the characters, whom he empties of emotion the better to express their passion. He explores their thoughts with the insistent

From *Cronaca di un Amore,* with Lucia Bose and Massimo Girotti.

"The luxurious interiors and the elegant costumes of the star, Lucia Bose, contrast with the sordid exteriors and the rainy, nocturnal atmosphere of the Milanese suburb...."

"These contrasts...set the lovers in opposition to each other..."

action of a camera that has become, in his hands, a surgical instrument. The director was to develop this method to a far greater degree in his later films, and especially in *Il Grido*.

It is also possible to find in *Cronaca di un Amore* other characteristic features of Antonioni. Like Ingmar Bergman, he is a woman's director. It is she—the Woman—who interests him more than anything else, she and her mysteries, her problems, her social evolution. It is she who nearly always determines the action or gives it its direction. In this film, the heroine contemplates homicide and leads her lover toward it. In *La Signora senza Camelie*, the woman is at the center of the drama. *Le Amiche* is entirely devoted to women, to their winning of material and moral independence. Even *Il Grido* is the tale of a man's despair seen through the women he meets on his anguished journey. As the Italian critic Fabio Carpi has emphasized, Antonioni has turned the heroine into a new kind of character in the Italian cinema, and even, one might say, in the cinema of the entire world. The woman has become an autonomous character; she is no longer designed to serve as a complement to one or more partners: that is to say, deformed by the domination of a masculine figure.

In this respect, Antonioni's work has a particularly modern feel. "I always give a great deal of importance to the feminine characters because I believe that I know women better than I do men. I think that reality can be filtered better through women's psychologies. They are more instinctive, more sincere."[6]

Was the predominance he grants to women not one of the reasons for the lack of success of Antonioni's early works? Centuries of theater and literature, decades of films, had imposed the idea of male primacy on the European public to such an extent that any departure from it, even before a public which considers itself extremely sophisticated, will disconcert the spectator. Although the evolution of the middle-class Western woman has created distressing problems and new situations, film makers before Antonioni ignored their existence. The psychological effects, in particular, were disregarded—one would think that there were no problems. The role of women in Antonioni's films is an important one. We shall return to it in our discussion of *Le Amiche*.

Antonioni was to concern himself next with a more specialized although equally timely theme—that of the amorality of postwar youth. *I Vinti* is composed of three stories, set in Rome, Paris and London. Together they form an inquest into, or testimony on, the moral distress of a disoriented younger generation.

The various episodes were based on actual events. Antonioni went to London and Paris to shoot the episodes that took place there; he used English and French actors respectively, and filmed each episode in its original tongue. All three parts ran into censorship trouble.

The English episode presents an unbalanced youth who writes poetry; he kills a prostitute partly because he considers her a source of evil and partly from his desire for fame. By considerable effort, he finally gets himself arrested and is put on trial—happy at last to be the center of attention. This episode was not allowed to be shown in England.

The French story was based on an actual incident involving juvenile delinquents known as the "J 3 of Malnoue." Alain Cuny was assistant director, and the film was shot in the streets, the subway, and at the Porte de Vincennes in Paris. Government authorization for shooting the picture had been granted with the reservation that the film's plot should differ sufficiently from the true story of the Malnoue delinquents. A French firm was at the time one of the co-producers. But the fact that French juvenile delinquency was being used as the subject of a film by an Italian director soon had the local press aroused, and even before the episode was finished, the French government forbade the export of either a negative or a working copy to Italy. This was apparently in accordance with the attorney general's policy of vetoing any film which deals with a court trial involving living persons— a somewhat paradoxical scruple in a country where the press gives criminal cases wide publicity, and even assumes guilt before it is proved. Permission to export the film to Italy was finally obtained, but its showing in France was forbidden and remains so today.

The original scenario for the Italian episode, "Uno dei Nostri Figli," told the story of a young Fascist who longs for the bygone "glory" of Mussolini's time. But the Government refused to sub-

From the French episode in *I Vinti*, with Etchika
Choureau and Jean-Pierre Mocky.

sidize this script, which is included in the present volume. The episode in *I Vinti* presents, instead, a youth of good background who, in a spirit of adventure, joins a gang of dope peddlers. He is pursued by the police in a nightmarish chase; a girl tries to help him, but he is finally killed. Antonioni still feels that this episode betrayed his original intent.

I Vinti was presented at the Venice Film Festival, but out of competition, because the French and English episodes had been dubbed. This was, in any case, unfortunate for a film of this type, which should have retained its original form as direct testimony.

André Bazin, who saw the film in Venice, wrote:

"The three parts are of uneven quality, and the Italian part could have been done by any fairly talented director, but the French is excellent and the English admirable. In them, an extreme purity of stylized realism is achieved, stripped of anything derivative in the editing and of every attempt at plastic seduction in the photography."[7]

In another article, the same critic spelled out the author's intentions:

"For Antonioni, it was a question of demonstrating an illness common to the whole of postwar European youth: a type of romanticism based on the idea of absurd and desperate action."

I Vinti takes a rather marginal place among the author's narrative works because of its "psychological-documentary" aspect. He has depicted youth's contemporary dilemma, in different countries and different social environments, in a tone so faithful to each of the countries that certain critics have seen the film as a sort of pastiche: Cayatte's approach in the French episode, English "sick comedy" in the London one, etc. Perhaps Antonioni wished to efface himself in this way, so that the true experiences he was presenting might appear as they would to eyewitnesses. "My experiences, my opinions, my mistakes (which are the most personal part of my experience), will transmit my message if they are sincere," he once said.[8] By relying on the experiences of others, he made himself more like the director of an inquest than the teller of a tale.

This approach is even more evident in "Tentato Suicidio" ("Suicide Attempt"), one of the episodes in *L'Amore in Città* ("Love in

"Tentato Suicidio," from *L'Amore in Città*.

the City"), an unusual film project in which Antonioni participated. The original plan was to make a "magazine on film"; the idea was proposed by Cesare Zavattini, Riccardo Ghione and Marco Ferreri. The first issue—and the only one ever to appear—dealt with "love in the city." Zavattini, Fellini, Antonioni and several other directors contributed to it, each treating one aspect of the subject in his own way.

Antonioni said of his section, "Tentato Suicidio": "This episode has a story behind it. I made it out of friendship. I was asked to do it by someone to whom I owed a favor in return for one I received from him. The theme was told to me over the telephone; 'Suicides,' they said; so I did suicides. . . ."[9]

Antonioni wished his treatment to have an analyst's dryness and logic. In order to evoke the image of suicide accurately and to avoid any temptation to novelizing, he called on the survivors of unsuccessful suicide attempts and asked them to tell their stories before the camera. Brought together in front of a vast cyclorama in the cold emptiness of the studio, they answered a number of questions and then acted out the way they had attempted to destroy themselves.

The footage was edited and some of the stories had to be eliminated completely. As far as Antonioni was concerned, the problem here was less to create a work of art than to make an experiment from which he could later draw themes that would no doubt be richer than this reality.

He wrote: "As soon as I understood their complex form of exhibitionism, these suicide subjects no longer disturbed me. Most of them were happy to have tried to kill themselves, and to be there, to talk about it before the camera; they were happy to earn money in such a simple way. They even flirted a little among themselves. They tried to make me believe that they had wanted to die, that they had repeated the act several times over, and that, when all was said and done, it was bad luck for them not to have succeeded. More than that: they were ready to try it again, if they should find themselves in the same situation tomorrow.

"I am sure that this is not true. I am sure that they were exaggerating through some inexplicable form of vanity and masochism. Such cases lie in the province of the psychologist, not the moralist.

I do not feel compelled to accept the idea that if a person commits suicide it is to some degree the fault of all of us. Suicide is such an enigmatic act, and it has existed everywhere, as long as man has existed. We can examine it from many points of view: the anatomical, the physiopathological, the statistical and sociological, the psychological. If it is true that suicide has a moral value and that psychology cannot ignore morality, it is no less true that morality cannot ignore the teachings of psychology. It has been written that suicide is an act of total psychology—which means that each suicide has its own story behind it. The captain who goes down with his ship is considered a hero, and society honors such heroes. The Church grants the sacraments to suicides who are judged to be mad. Thus we cannot draw an abstract principle and ignore particular causes."[10]

Despite this intellectual approach, there is something very disturbing in Antonioni's film, in the monotonous, almost stunned, tone of the suicides as they relate their stories. The total effect is more morbid than edifying. But no matter how we may feel about it, this bold vision of the role that the cinema can sometimes play surely deserves our respect.

"I sought to arouse the public's revulsion against suicide by showing the spiritual desolation of the characters," Antonioni points out.

Before shooting this sketch for *L'Amore in Città*, Antonioni returned to the narrative line he had begun with *Cronaca di un Amore*—this time with a film which was certainly less revealing, and which remains, in spite of some of its high points, the least exciting in his career. *La Signora senza Camelie*, like *I Vinti*, was co-produced by an Italian and a French firm. It was eventually released in Italy and in France (in France under the title *Corps sans Âme*), but it had little commercial success. It earned more money in France, however, than in Antonioni's own country.

The making of the film itself had its ups and downs. The subject was originally conceived for Gina Lollobrigida, but she refused to play a part which too closely resembled herself. Antonioni then thought of Sophia Loren but was unable to obtain her services, and it was to Lucia Bose, of *Cronaca*, that the role, which was not particularly suitable for her, finally fell. She played it with great

Lucia Bose, in *La Signora senza Camelie*.

talent nonetheless. The character suggested the careers of many actresses, especially in Italy: "A *ragazza* raised among the common people, who wins a beauty contest and is launched like a paper boat into a diabolical whirlpool, where, like a character out of Pirandello, she searches in vain for her own identity. . . . She is the victim of no one, only of her own destiny."[11]

The external aspects of the film probably detract from its deeper theme and incline us to do it an injustice. But we can pick out the director's major preoccupations behind the ridiculous behavior of the actress and certain weaknesses in the plot. We find Antonioni's favorite leitmotiv in the isolation against which the heroine carries on her vain struggle. "This search," Marcel Martin says, "takes place in a series of gropings, which give the story line the sinuosity and uncertainty that are so characteristic of Antonioni's scenarios —the improvised, unplanned feeling, the naturalness that comes so close to real life through the banality and the veracity of the characters' situations."[12]

The actress commits a form of suicide at the end of the film, when she accepts degrading roles in the carnival atmosphere of a film studio without any prestige. Disappointed in the glory that she has been unable to achieve, in the love that she has been unable to win, the *ragazza* returns to her mediocrity, but this time with an awareness of inescapable solitude.

An interesting comparison can be made between this film and another on which Antonioni was working at about the same time —*Lo Sceicco Bianco* ("The White Sheik"), directed by Fellini. In both, the characters struggle in a world built on phoniness and artifice. Both are something more than illustrations of an absurd truth: they are the very reflection of that truth. The world of movie-making and that of the "novel-in-photographs" contain the same illusions and the same stupidities. The similarity of intention is clear, although their development diverges because of the differences in dramatic temperament between the two directors, Antonioni and Fellini. Working in the more classic form of the two, Antonioni subtly shifts from one genre to another, from satirical comedy to drama, each mood throwing light on the heroine's gradually increasing self-knowledge, up to the point where she discovers simultaneously the vanity of her own ambitions and the faithlessness, cowardice and weakness of those who surround her. Her final surrender plunges the satire into a mood of bitterness that foreshadows the director's later works.

This was in 1953. In the next six years Antonioni was to make only two films, but both were remarkable. Together they revealed the director's character and indicated the road he would take in the future.

3. Le Amiche

Having reached this stage in Antonioni's career, I should like to try to do something more than merely analyze individual films: to pick out the main currents that flow through and unify his work, to note the motifs that recur and develop.

In most of their external aspects, the two films that Antonioni made at two-year intervals after 1953—*Le Amiche* and *Il Grido*—are utterly different. Everything about them is different except the one thing that is deepest and most secret, the spirit of Antonioni himself. "The greatest purist, the most rigorous, the cleverest perhaps of the new Italian directors," André Bazin wrote, as early as 1952, in France.[1] "A moralist," we read elsewhere,[2] "who leans bitterly on the absurdity of life and, refusing both the attitudes of revolt and resignation, seeks a salvation which would have nothing metaphysical about it."

In *Le Amiche* we have a multifaceted story of several women in a frivolous setting: the social and artistic middle-class of Turin; in *Il Grido* the story of a laborer abandoned by the woman he loves, pursuing his impossible search for forgetfulness along the desolate roads of the Po valley. In *Le Amiche* a number of separate plots converge with multiple repercussions upon one another; in *Il Grido,* a kind of massive tide flows through episodes which have no connection save the presence of the hero, running toward death like a river flowing into the sea. Contrasting with the occasionally brilliant atmosphere and psychological subtleties of the first, we have the grayness of the winter countryside, the elementary drama of the lone man, in the second. At bottom, however, there is in both the same almost irremediable anguish, which is, in fact, the feeling of the soul's solitude, of man's desperate effort to rediscover himself beyond himself. It is in this light that *Il Grido*, which at first glance seems less rich, less complex than Antonioni's other films, appears to us, nevertheless, as the most finished, the film in which the author has attained the perfection of a masterpiece.

Carnal love is exposed in both works as an illusory remedy for human sadness, for the ultimate anxiety which—even more than unrequited love itself—leads Rosetta in *Le Amiche* to suicide and delivers the hero of *Il Grido* to the same fate.

Le Amiche is drawn from a story by Pavese, *Tra Donne Sole*, the last panel in a triptych of novellas by the Turinese writer. One of the greatest contemporary Italian novelists, Cesare Pavese himself committed suicide in 1955 at the age of forty-seven, when his works were just beginning to enjoy wide success, because he felt he had come to the end of what he could accomplish. Almost twenty years earlier, in 1937, Pavese wrote in his journal: "There is one thing sadder than to have failed in one's ideals—to have realized them." A bitter sentence but one which expresses a truth and explains, if it does not justify, his end.

Antonioni refers often and openly to the novelist, and there is a certain similarity between Pavese's work and that of the director—but a similarity much more complex than a case of Pavese's influencing Antonioni. The comparison must have flattered Antonioni at first; I have the feeling that today it irritates him. Certainly more than one literary influence has worked on the director's art. As far as influences are concerned, it is the sum total of Antonioni's wide reading that has guided his dramatic expression toward the "film-novel" which is sometimes considered his greatest contribution to contemporary cinema.

Antonioni's references to Pavese reveal what is essentially a deep identity of thought. The following remark in Pavese's journal might be regarded as summing up the central theme of Antonioni's work: "The whole problem of life is thus: how to break out of one's own solitude, how to communicate with others." Not one of the director's films disregards this underlying question. But when this much has been granted, it must be pointed out that there are as many divergences as likenesses between novelist and director. The first difference was defined by Antonioni himself: "Pavese committed suicide and I am still alive." However, it is above all in their ideas about women that they differ most sharply. All the love Antonioni bears toward women, all the happiness he offers them, is—by contrast—demanded of them by Pavese. The writer's bitterness lies in the impossibility of ever *obtaining* such happiness; for the director, it seems to be the impossibility of *giving* a woman happiness. "I understand man, with his faults and his virtues: those of many men I know, and no doubt my own as well," Antonioni has said. "But what I love first of all and above all is woman. Perhaps because I understand her better."[3]

In *Le Amiche,* the ambitions and the little intrigues do not refute this admiration of Antonioni for women. Compare the female characters with the men who surround them: they are superior, and in their very vanity they are straighter, truer in character. It may seem paradoxical—but it is not—that *Le Amiche,* although based on a Pavese story, is the least "Pavesian" of all Antonioni's works. Far less so than *Il Grido,* for example. The spirit of Pavese's *Tra Donne Sole* is very different from the film Antonioni made of it.

Antonioni himself has spoken out on this point: "I think I have read Pavese rather closely, but there are writers I like and respect more than I do him. What I liked in *Tra Donne Sole* were the female characters and their way of living out events internally. Besides, one of the characters bore an extraordinary resemblance to someone whom I knew only too well in real life; I wanted to talk about her and present her."[4]

The problem of adaptation which had to be resolved was then, from the very beginning, more extensive than one of mere cinematographic transposition. In the first place, the story lacked any plot; it was a twisted skein of incidents out of which a drama must be spun. In the second, Antonioni wished to insert several personal "experiences" of his own and of his collaborators. Two women assisted in the adaptation: Suso Cecchi d'Amico and Alba de Cespedes. The former, one of the most active of Italian scenarists, did the basic work; the latter, a novelist of international reputation, wrote the dialogue. One worked in the daytime, the other at night, so that they partically never met in the course of their collaboration.

"Antonioni," Alba de Cespedes told me, "was the bond between us. As is customary with him, he said nothing about the things he wanted done, although he knew precisely what they were; he brought the two of us around to his views by switching us onto his train of thought." But what Antonioni expected from his collaborators above all was their own experiences, with which he intended to modify and "dramatize" the original story.

The film credits specify, "Freely adapted from the novel by Pavese." The film is, in fact, an original creation. The two stories are as different as the forms in which they are expressed. Like many of my colleagues, I read the book after having seen the film, and then saw the film again. The complexity of the film, which is particularly striking the first time one sees it—and which is one of its key merits—clarifies after a reading of the literary work, and in a most singular way. Of course the characters are different in the film; some disappear, others are added; but, more than anything else, their motives are clarified. We shall say no more on this point, except to call the reader's attention to the article by Jacques Doniol-Valcroze on page 149, which deals in particular with it.

By providing more precise dramatic motivation in a more closely woven plot, by relating Rosetta's suicide more directly to its causes, the director has not, however, diminished his theme. These emotional subthemes are powerless to dominate the major subject: the anguish inherent in life itself.

I shall speak later of Michelangelo Antonioni's position in relation to neorealism, but here, as in *Cronaca di un Amore,* we can plainly see, apart from the middle-class environment which was so often neglected by the representatives of that school, several things which are clearly the director's own personal contribution. The atmosphere and the settings *reflect* the characters to a far greater degree than they *define* them. It is through the characters, the behavior of human beings, that the world around them—built in the image of their own vanity—is depicted. These characters are not the victims of an environment, nor are they even influenced by it, like some of Rossellini's; they *form* the setting of their own lives, as the spider spins its web, enclosing themselves within a net from which they draw subsistence but in which they finally become prisoners. Entwined in their weaknesses, they can find no escape save in cynicism, despair or voluntary death. Work and love—because they are inaccessible or insufficient—are nothing more than palliatives, and then only for those whose will is strong enough to grasp hold of them.

Because the characters dominate the action in this way, the plot or—to be more precise as far as *Le Amiche* is concerned—the plots, are spun and reach their climaxes without making the principal claim on the spectator's attention. Rather, they compose a series of variations on a major theme; they illustrate the characters' psychologies, whereas in most other films they would explain them. Here is the great novelty in Antonioni's work—what Doniol-Valcroze calls "an attempt to substitute for the cinema-as-spectacle a cinema of behavior and of interiority, to set in motion an evolution toward a more mature form."

In Antonioni's work there is never a question of crises but of states of being. Feelings and passions affect, carry along with them, the movement of life. The intensity of the internal drama is contrasted with the commonplaces of everyday life, as in this film, for instance, in the fashion show that follows the young woman's suicide. Because there are no crises but rather states of being and feeling, nothing is ever brought to a climax, nor is a problem ever resolved. Rosetta's weakness, her incapacity for living without some support, Momina's cynicism, the artist's pride, the greed of some, the vanity of others, meet, clash, are mutually destroyed. And life goes on.

Here, once again, the form is that of a chronicle rather than a story; the severe tone excludes sentimental effects, dramatic crescendos. The quality of the expression, the severity itself, confer on this work its principal attraction. The black magic of Antonioni's first film returns here, multiplied in the many-faceted mirror which intersects and multiplies the images of the women's faces.

The subject required it, of course, but the superiority of the feminine to the masculine portraits in *Le Amiche* is as striking as in the director's more recent works. Never before had the screen presented us, simultaneously, with such a number of authoritatively depicted characters, so true in their diversity and in their

From *Le Amiche:*
(Above) Eleonora Rossi-Drago and Yvonne Furneaux.
(Below) Maddalena Fischer, Yvonne Furneaux and
Anna Maria Pancani (standing); Valentina Cortese and
Eleonora Rossi-Drago (seated).

contradictions, as those of this set of "friends." What an astonishing range there is, running from cruelty to tenderness, each character drawn with equal skill! . . .

Rosetta, with her weakness, her ignorance, her need for love to reveal her to herself, her pitiful tenderness, her tendency to make a fool of herself, her pride (her attitude when she has become Lorenzo's mistress), the vanity of her playing a role for which she is not suited and which will shatter her. "An idiot," Momina says with her usual cruel lucidity.

Clelia, with her cool head, her knowledge of what she wants and where she is going. Sensitive, true, human, though never allowing herself to be dominated by her feelings, her desires, or even her ambitions. She is not afraid to jeopardize her career by crying out the truth that is smothering her. But she does refuse the love that would force her to abdicate her own personality, the love of a man who is not her social equal.

Nene, as lucid in her pity as Momina in her pride and Clelia in her loves.

And, especially, Momina, so admirably conceived and played by Yvonne Furneaux—living in the midst of the intrigues of the others, provoking, complicating and resolving them with sadistic joy, with the pleasure of a cat; sure of herself, of her toughness, of her terrible emotional balance—qualities which are not in the least contradicted by her shedding a few tears, tears of rage more than of humiliation.

All of them, down to the blond Mariella—who is played in a minor key but is nevertheless as true as the others in her innocent stupidity—compose a portrait gallery of which the best novelist would not be ashamed. On this merry-go-round of wild female tigers, their claws all more or less sharpened, the men come off as rather pitiful figures. This does not mean that they are monotonous or boring. Ferzetti, in particular, gives us an accurate portrait of the failed artist, a portrait which we are to see again, presented by the same actor, in *L'Avventura*.

So much novelty in the conception of the film called for an equivalent in its form. The need Antonioni has expressed "to follow his characters," the going and coming, the interlacing of vari-

The beach sequence,
Le Amiche.

ous lives, the chance encounters, give the film an extraordinary rhythm. "You will not find a single example of action-reaction (reverse camera angle) shooting in *Le Amiche*," he said to the students at the Experimental Film Center in Rome. "This technique expresses nothing." The scenes are long, there are many sequences; Antonioni insisted on scenes as inactive, as free of actual events, as possible. Such events as do occur are always presented with admirable restraint, as in the case of Rosetta's suicide —the waterfront viewed from a distance, the hearse, the shroud.

One of the sequences which has become famous, that of the walk along the seashore—a sequence most stage-oriented directors would consider useless—sums up and expresses the whole film with arresting poetry and bitterness. Antonioni, who has often been contrasted with Fellini, here joins hands with the director of *I Vitelloni*. It is when they escape from the world, which (like the spider) they have secreted from their own pores, that Antonioni's heroines appear stripped of externals, just as the *vitelloni*, faced with the solitude and vastness of a similar wintry, windswept beach, first become conscious of the meaninglessness of their lives.

It is not surprising that Antonioni ran into opposition in putting across such a bitter message. For he was depicting in *Le Amiche* not only the desolation of private human relationships but also a social class whose vanity and uselessness were bringing about its own disintegration. Financial troubles interrupted work on the film for several months; the same thing was to happen with *Il Grido*. "You cannot imagine," he said to me in 1958, "what difficulties we have to surmount in Italy, not to make a good film but to make any film at all." And on a later occasion: "I love none of my films, or at least I have no particular predilection for any one among them. This is because I have never been able to make a film under normal conditions, expressing everything I wanted to express. All my films leave me unsatisfied. When I see them again, there is always something that irritates me, precisely because I remember the difficulties I had to face, and I am furious at myself for not having known how to surmount them more effectively."[5]

Le Amiche, with its unusual density, did not break through the barrier of public incomprehension outside Italy, despite the fact that it received a prize at the Venice Film Festival. Nor was *Il*

Grido, with its deeper and more directly expressed emotion, to bring him public acceptance.

4. Il Grido

The original idea for *Il Grido* goes back to the time when Antonioni was collaborating on De Santis' *Caccia Tragica* in Tuscany and Emilia. In the autumn of 1954 he presented his idea to various producers—unsuccessfully. Abandoning the project, he set to work on *Le Amiche.* Nearly two years later, the producer Franco Cancellieri proposed that the director resume work on his earlier idea. The completion of the scenario and the search for locations consumed the summer of that year.

At the beginning of autumn, the assembled cast and crew set up headquarters in Ferrara. The shooting was to be done in the lower Po valley, on the border between Emilia and Venezia.

Il Grido occupies a very special place among Antonioni's works, representing both a climax and a certain kind of exception. It has deep psychological links with his other films. But, for the first and only time—if we leave aside the documentaries, which were indeed forerunners to *Il Grido*—the director abandoned the middle class. He chose a worker for his hero and presented throughout the film situations involving working people. Yet in *Il Grido* the characters' social position is transcended to a greater degree than in any of Antonioni's other films. Antonioni detaches the hero from his particular world and places him in a sort of no man's land, out of time and space. *Il Grido* demonstrates that the director's scope extends beyond any single social condition or period. His subject is man himself.

Briefly, the film tells the story of a man, Aldo, abandoned by the woman he loves, Irma. His life is shattered and he departs, fleeing the thing that has been both the framework and the condition of his destiny. His adventures, his encounters with other women, cannot free him from the memory of a love that has become part of his own flesh, his own thought. When he comes back and witnesses the happiness that she has found apart from him, the man abandons himself to a death, the cause of which—dizziness or suicide?—the director purposely leaves ambiguous. It does not matter; whether voluntary or not, the hero's fall into space is the only way out of his circular dilemma.

In *Il Grido,* Antonioni presents us with neither a plot nor characters, but primarily and essentially with a thought. The subject is a double one, or, to be more accurate, it lies on two juxtaposed planes. It is the theme of absolute love which binds the life of one human being to that of another so closely that a rupture between them is equivalent to annihilation. And since this love requires a kind of miracle in order to endure and to remain fully shared, the theme thus broadens into that of human solitude—not simply in the terms in which that solitude has so often been expressed, but an original, fundamental solitude resulting from the rupture of a natural entity: the couple. It is astonishing that Catholic critics have not looked beyond the "sin" of this unmarried couple and seized upon their love, which is presented in all its ideal spirituality.

There hardly exists a single work, particularly on the screen, which presents such a lofty conception of the human being, which endows him with such individuality—composed of flesh and blood, of course, but formed in the image of God—unique, indefinable, irreplaceable. Aldo, separated from Irma, does not bury himself in voluntary despair; he does not question himself, does not feed a sadness which, in any case, still remains unformulated. It is not true that Aldo has "made up his mind not to find the happiness he pretends to be seeking."[1] Antonioni himself makes this clear: "Previously my charaacters often took pleasure in their difficulties and in their sentimental crises. This time we are dealing with a man who reacts, who seeks to break through his unhappiness. Thus, I have treated this character with much more pity."[2]

Aldo wants to go on living, but in a different way, in different surroundings, by different means, since the whole of his past life is bound up with Irma's presence. This motivates his vagabondage, which is simultaneously a flight, a quest for a new love, a new job, and a quest for oblivion as the condition for a new life. He is to perform new tasks, he is to know other women, all of whom, like Irma, can give him sexual pleasure, security, the simple happiness of being alive. . . . But they are not the being originally "bestowed" upon him, the unique being; and this fact alone is enough to make his love, like his work, like his days, joyless, vain and empty.

Therefore, Aldo's despair is total and irremediable. When he has completed the long journey that leads him to the depths of despair, to the cabin in the Po delta soon to be threatened by the rising waters, the solitary figure suddenly turns back and, without stopping, retraces the road he has just traveled, as if eager to confront the final evidence of his misfortune. He climbs up once more to the refinery tower, from which, as he says, "I could see my house, the river, my daughter . . . ," the whole of his modest universe, the things which made him *himself* and not anyone else. Oblivion does not only kill the one who is forgotten, but also the one who forgets. Irma may perhaps have become someone other than the person she was, Aldo cannot. There is no longer any place for him except in non-being.

Critics have complained that his death is not moving and that the film as a whole is "cold." But his death is simply *necessary;* it is an inevitable climax, lying beyond the range of feelings. I have seen *Il Grido* at least a half dozen times now and have uncovered new depths of emotion with each viewing—which is quite the opposite of what usually happens. The fact is that the emotion in *Il Grido* does not derive from events but rather from our comprehension of the drama through which the hero lives. If the same phenomenon can be noted in Chaplin's films, it is for precisely the same reason: the emotion lies within the character and not in the actions he performs or the incidents in which he is involved. In *Il Grido,* emotion takes hold when the action is suspended. This occurs in several places—for example, after the *motoscafo* race when Aldo suddenly stops, alone and apart. We see him almost directly from behind and out of his immobility there rises, like nausea, the feeling of despair.

Thus it is the thought which creates the drama, arouses emotion, makes the characters act. Aldo, the main character, becomes—from the moment when the rupture with his mistress takes place—no more than the filament through which the film's emotional current is conducted. He is the leitmotiv about which his various female partners, the environments into which he wanders, and the events

in which he is involved play in counterpoint. Because Aldo's story
is the drama of a thought, it seems to be, more than Antonioni's
other works, a film about Man rather than a particular man. With
the same kind of interiority, Chaplin was able to turn a very specific character into a universal symbol. *Il Grido* is not Aldo's story
but the drama of a man destined to solitude. It rises from the level
of sentimentality to that of moral distress.

Superficially the film may seem diffuse and full of irrelevant incident. Actually it has a remarkable cohesiveness. Let us go back
over the structure of the film to see how Antonioni binds it together, image by image, and how he relates episode to theme.

The film's action opens at the moment when Aldo comes down
from the tower of the refinery where he works. At the same time,
Irma, who has just brought his lunch pail to the factory, turns
back to her house. This double movement in opposite directions
marks the rupture between the couple. Antonioni tells us little
about the reasons for the rupture—he will show only its effects; but
we already know that the break is final and inevitable, and we
know this in part just because the true cause is never explained.
What we see is two human beings separating, a unity dissolving.

While the break rips away at their emotions, life goes on around
them; the neighbors, Irma's sister, Aldo's mother, the shopkeepers,
proceed along their parallel paths. In the house at the river's edge,
which is to hold them together only a little longer, Aldo watches
Irma as she moves about making her everyday gestures, the gestures of a life that has already lost its meaning and is soon to come
to an end. At this point, Aldo becomes conscious that the reality
of his life is now a thing of the past, that he is lost. Nevertheless,
he tries to hold on to her; side by side, the two of them play out a
game of hide-and-seek, searching in each other for justification,
for illusory aid, until the moment when Aldo performs the brutal
act which finally frees Irma and, up to a certain point, justifies the
rupture in her eyes and in those of the neighbors. Aldo leaves, taking their daughter, Rosina, with him, and she becomes the witness
to his solitude while also remaining a last link between him and
Irma.

This first part of the film is circular, the couple's drama radiating
out in all directions, touching the community, the relatives, the vil-

From *Il Grido*.
"...the break rips away at
their emotions..."

The slapping scene. Aldo
(Steve Cochran) and Irma
(Alida Valli)

lagers, until the slapping scene casts Irma and Aldo outside the world that united them and onto an unknown trajectory. From this moment forward, the composition is totally changed. We hardly see Irma again until the final scene. It is Aldo alone who now engages our interest, because the film is his story, but more importantly because he is the one who is faithful to his absolute love and because that love destines him henceforward to solitude.

Antonioni projects his drama in a long, gray, muted tonality, a slow and steady progression, as neutral in appearance as the heavy gray water of the River Po down which the hero makes his lonely way. Around this linear motif, the film's internal theme, are gathered a number of external motifs—episodes which might seem unrelated to that central theme but which actually give it its real size and scope. The *motoscafo* race, the customers at the service station, the friends on the dredger, and particularly, at the end, the extraordinary sequence of the villagers' demonstration—all these bear witness, with mounting intensity, to Aldo's detachment, to the degree to which he has become a stranger to everything that does not concern his own inner drama. He is isolated in the midst of his peers. His participation in events grows progressively less active, indicating the decreasing interest he takes in everything that surrounds him. He repairs the *motoscafo,* watches the race for a moment; he takes Virginia's place at the gas pump for a time; he questions the dredgers, suddenly dreams of escape. His relation to the external world still manifests itself up to a certain point in his behavior. The fact that he takes Rosina along with him on the first part of his exodus is better explained by her constituting a last link with Irma than by any affection the father feels for the child.

Yet Antonioni makes Rosina emerge as an individual. She lives parallel with her father but also has her own personal life amid all the events that occur during their journey: the encounter with the madmen[3] and with the school children, her friendship with Virginia's old father, who is threatened in the same way as she—by the love struggling to emerge before their eyes. Little is said about Rosina; she has practically no lines to speak, no scene to play, but she *exists,* and with an intensity that enriches her presence as the last link between Aldo and Irma. When Aldo sends her away to

Il Grido:
(Above) Rosina with her father, Aldo.
(Below) "...alienation of the feelings..." Aldo and
Andreina (Lyn Shaw)

school, this link is broken and the bitterness becomes unbearable.

The last episode in Aldo's wandering, the sequence with Andreina set against the frightful misery of the delta fishermen, shows him to us defeated, annihilated. When he returns to his former world, he finds that he is a stranger there, an unknown man. The external action at this point takes the form of a drama, a collective drama which all the inhabitants of the village—who have been threatened with expropriation—are experiencing. But Aldo carries on with his solitary quest, making his lonely way through the very midst of the crowd on their way to the protest meeting.

The long journey he has made through the wintry mist has taught him that the empty place left by Irma in his life and in his heart can never be filled by anything else. Not by another love, nor by pleasure, nor by action, nor by rancor, nor by hatred. Glimpsing Irma as a happy wife and mother does not really change anything; it is only a confirmation. At the last limit of his misery, he is without scorn or desire. There is nothing left of him.

In his ultimate loneliness, Aldo climbs up the tower in the courtyard of the factory, deserted by his former comrades, all of whom have answered the call to collective action. What he can see from up above no longer belongs to him. He is rejected, lost. His gesture of farewell is to Irma standing below, but also to his own bit of countryside, to his life.

Irma tries to reach him; all that is left for her to do is to gather up his corpse. Along with this image of the couple destroyed— this time in the physical sense too—we see the people rushing to their meeting. The collective drama is joined to the individual drama, but does not mix with it. Aldo has died alone.

Thus the internal power of the film is almost never expressed dramatically, but rather through the symphonic character of the film's construction and through the close unity between the characters and their physical surroundings.

This construction has a musical form, with its melodic line, its parallel motifs, its restatements of themes. The drama opens and closes on the same high note—the verticality of the tower where Aldo appears at the very beginning and from which he falls at the end. The images that lead up to it (during the credits) and return us to it at the end are accompanied by a theme for violin and orchestra, the only orchestral theme in the film. At other times, silence is broken only by a leitmotiv played on the piano, a few notes of despairing and discreet bitterness which accompany the memory of Irma in the solitary hero's thoughts.

Perhaps no other film has given a better demonstration of the cohesiveness that the cinema can achieve. Never, at any event, have the contributions of the cameraman and the musical director been of such crucial importance. At the same time, *Il Grido* has a kind of classic spareness which seems to set it apart from Antonioni's other works. Actually, this spareness conceals a complexity of theme, structure and expression that is revolutionary. *Il Grido* is, indeed, a classic of cinematography, and certainly one of the most significant films of recent years, marking a clear break between narrative and poetic cinema. This last term is used in the sense of a transcendence of the thing presented, whether from an artistic or philosophical or psychological viewpoint. It is clear that two works as easy to contrast as *Il Grido* and *French Cancan,* for example, still belong to the same family and depend on the same hierarchy of values, from which we must exclude works constructed on stricter dramatic or psychological principles.

The environment of *Il Grido* and its general tonality have elicited facile comparisons with neorealism. But if *Il Grido* can be linked with that school, it is only as a climax to it and a renovation of it. A climax because Antonioni has used with intense purity the dominant elements of neorealism: truth of feeling, simplicity of action, a humanistic theme, a setting marked by poverty and dreariness. No neorealistic work has gone so deep into despair. *Il Grido* is a harrowing film, more harrowing than *Umberto D.* It is also a renovation because beyond the dramatic elements, beyond the journey through the winter mud and the various encounters, beyond the anguish, there is the miracle of a sympathetic magic, a poetic charm. One critic has called this quality "musical," and this is accurate. It seizes the spectator quite independently of any psychological meaning or formal quality.

Like all Antonioni's films, *Il Grido* is a statement of fact. He faces us with human beings whose behavior he follows with the lucidity—we are tempted to say "clinical" lucidity—which has often earned him the accusation of coldness. He does not participate in his characters' drama; he watches them, in order to deliver them over to us. Thus we are perfectly free not only to judge them but to understand them. It is the mark of the great artist that he leaves a man free before his creations, that he does not load them with a preconceived moral. The creation lives to the extent to which it admits the greatest number of varied—and even contradictory—interpretations.

Of all Antonioni's films, *Il Grido* is the richest in possible meanings. Here is a picture of a man dominated by events, by fatality, against which he does his best to struggle. Depending on the spectator's turn of mind, the man is either a pitiful figure, the victim of his own weakness, or a hero, in the ancient sense of the term, through the very force of the destiny that overwhelms him.

The film's emotion, the long sob it breathes from beginning to end, goes far beyond the feelings expressed, far beyond the story of a love, no matter how absolute. It is an awareness of the human condition, man torn forever between aspiration and the mutability that constitutes his limitation. It is the tragedy of the "inability to communicate" between human beings, expressed not merely through one particular case but in its most specific form, the entity of the couple—two elements which can melt completely into one another only by abolishing their original selves.

Pavese has written a sentence which conveys the meaning of *Il Grido:* "One does not kill oneself out of love *for* a woman. One kills oneself because a love, any love at all, reveals us in our nakedness, in our misery, in our most defenseless state, in our non-being."

It would be more accurate, perhaps, to say that this revelation occurs when love strips off the mask that it has itself placed over the nakedness, over the non-being. Because the very achievement of absolute love leaves those who feel it nothing more than ashes and vanity. Such is the case with Rosetta in *Le Amiche*—and with Aldo. Once their love is broken, nothing is left of them; they aspire to the physical non-being which alone can eradicate their moral non-being.

Thus we see that the very exaltation of love produces its terrible opposite: the tragic dependency of the man who is affected by it. In the peaceful happiness which composed his former life, Aldo did not see that he had abdicated from everything that made him the man he was; that his taste for life, his work, his pleasures, his moments of quiet, no longer belonged to him but were bound up in Irma's presence. Bound up not in the external things that she provided—love, security, the reality of his home, all the "replaceable" things—but in *herself*, her irreducible individuality, her, the irreplaceable. What causes his distress, what makes him so pitiful and so human in our eyes, is not the loss of a woman but the impossibility of freeing himself from her memory, of once again becoming himself.

Is total love then granted to a man only at the highest price, the price of his liberty? This is the question presented by *Il Grido*.

There has been much talk about the fragility of the emotions in Antonioni's later films. Here, on the contrary, we are dealing with their all-powerfulness. And it is all the more striking because they are the feelings of simple people whose sincerity is not affected by social or psychological influences. The tragic theme may thus be regarded, from an ethical stand, as the indictment of a condition which reduces a man by depriving him of his liberty—his energy, his will, his vital force.

One critic has followed this line of thought and considered *Il Grido* as a critique rather than an exaltation of emotion. Gerard Gozlan, in his elaborate Marxist study[4] writes:

"If, in the year 1960, any individual, no matter who he may be, feels such bewilderment, such absence of freedom, such inability to choose, to stand at a distance from his own feelings and so to repress them . . . if, in the year 1960, an individual can be a prisoner of his feelings in this way, then the concept of love that society has taught him is a corrupt one; then it is as necessary to call our civilization into question for the way it deals with the feelings as it is for economic and political reasons. . . . Here is the scandal: a man kills himself because a woman has left him. A man kills himself out of love—there is the contradiction. On this same point, Brecht spoke of a 'crisis of sensitivity,' a crisis pointing up our decayed traditions and the fact that there is a whole range of feelings no longer attuned to reality."

Gozlan finds support for his argument in the statement (included in this book, p. 90) that Antonioni wrote as a preface to the presentation of *L'Avventura* at the Cannes festival.

"*Il Grido* is not, as many like to say, a film glorifying eternal love, but, plainly and simply, a critical film, in which the hero is neither weak nor impotent, but merely alienated [in the Brechtian sense]. *Il Grido* is a film about the alienation of the feelings. Let us make no mistake about the way in which Antonioni regards his character. It is perfectly normal that this film should at first appear to be a film about love. And in fact, such as it is, it is one of the most beautiful films ever made about love. On this we will agree. But the power and the scope of this film about love lie in the fact that it forces us to reflect on our concepts of love: our madly-in-loves, our passionate loves, our sentimental loves, etc."

That social evolution should bring man to the point where he considers the possibility or necessity of revising his feelings is clear enough. But will the external conditions of existence be capable of exerting an influence on man's happiness, on his equilibrium? These new conditions will create new problems, will involve man in a new web of dependencies. Where will they lead him? No one can answer this question. "We have not been able to find any new feelings," writes Antonioni, "nor even to get an inkling of a solution to this problem. I do not pretend to be able to find this solution. I am not a moralist."

5. L'Avventura

The two works that followed *Il Grido* were to mark an evolution in Antonioni's art—an evolution, not a rupture or a revolution. All the boldness to be found in *L'Avventura* and *La Notte* was already there, in embryo, in the earlier works, beginning with *Cronaca di un Amore*. But Antonioni now goes beyond a dramatic statement of fact and, in both the later films, sketches a proposed solution to the anguish of existence. This solution has been summed up in a remark the director once made about his characters: "They are saved to the degree to which there is established between them a link founded on reciprocal pity, on understanding, and on a resignation which is not weakness but the only power that will allow them to remain together, to be bound together for life, to oppose catastrophe."[1] Here again a parallel course in the disintegration of the feelings is presupposed, although, paradoxically, it maintains a certain unity within the couple. This possibility of pity, of resignation, could not save Aldo.

The fact that *Il Grido* did not enjoy commercial success was doubtless one of the reasons that, during the winter of 1957-58, Antonioni renewed his activities in the theater. With Elio Bartolini, co-scenarist of *Il Grido,* he wrote a play called *Scandali Segreti,* formed a company and directed the play at the Eliseo Theater in Rome. Then came a road tour through Italy, followed by the production of Van Druten's *I Am a Camera* with the same company. The leading lady was Monica Vitti, who had already worked with Antonioni on *Il Grido,* dubbing for Dorian Gray.

Financial difficulties arose, and the company was dissolved. Antonioni then returned to his film projects. "Directing for the theater bores me because of its many conventions. I believe I really am exclusively a man of the cinema," he now says.

During the summer of 1958, Antonioni was working on a scenario entitled *Makaroni,* a story of Italian prisoners in Germany. (Incidentally, this is a subject about which he has not stopped thinking; he says that the film, as he conceives it, differs widely from everything he has done up to now.) The project was fairly advanced; shooting was to begin in a few weeks. But the producer, Enzo Merolle, failed to sign a final contract with Antonioni, who then lost interest.

Antonioni's next film—*L'Avventura*—was born out of a meeting with Gino Rossi, who had been production manager of *Cronaca di un Amore.* Rossi was enthusiastic about the new film and wanted to produce it, but after two weeks of shooting he dropped out. This was only the beginning of the many problems that were to plague the making of *L'Avventura.*

Antonioni had shot all his previous films in the north of Italy. He once said: "I would feel ill at ease if I had to do any shooting in the south, for the people who live there are too different from me. I can never understand them." Antonioni seeks out melancholy atmospheres—gray tones and overcast skies—because they are in harmony with his own spirit and with the subjects he treats. There is also another reason: "The sun's position forces me to shoot from a certain angle. When the sun is behind me, there is a camera shadow; when it is opposite, sunlight enters the camera and dictates the camera angle and the shots. Since one of the things that preoccupies me is the possibility of following a character for a long stretch of time, it is obvious that the lack of sun allows me to do this more easily."[2]

When he set the action of *L'Avventura* in Sicily, Antonioni did no more than create a new framework for his plot, a plot that was wholly foreign to its setting. The characters, all Romans, were to find in their unaccustomed environment a further cause for the disorder of their own feelings—much like the characters of *Le Amiche* on their deserted beach. Antonioni was to draw from this sun-baked island of volcanic ash a kind of ideal, even abstract, solitude, the concrete form of which was expressed in landscapes of rocks and foaming water bathed in a cold, gray light.

The misadventures which occurred during the film's production have been recorded in a book by Tommaso Chiaretti, *L'Avventura di Michelangelo Antonioni*. The shooting took several months, partly because of difficulties always present in outdoor work, partly because of financial problems which, in this case, reached the point where the production company (Imeria) went bankrupt. Cast and crew were left without funds, without news from Rome, stranded on an island where they continued the make-believe re-creation of a summer cruise on into the dead of winter. Antonioni had to face grumbling and strikes and creditors while waiting for Cino Del Duca to take over production, thereby enabling him to finish. Shooting was finally completed on January 15, 1960.

Four months later, the film was shown at the Cannes Festival. This première, held in the large auditorium of the Festival Palace with the director and his cast present, set off a chorus of shouting and whistling, a hue and cry unlike anything seen since the showing of Carné's *Juliette*. Antonioni had concrete confirmation of the public's incomprehension—a state of affairs that might well have been considered irremediable.

The critics, however, were unanimous in recognizing *L'Avventura* as an exceptionally important work, a film that went far beyond the cinema as it had thus far evolved. (See the "Statement for *L'Avventura*," p. 183.) But many of them considered it suitable at present only for a special audience. Several critics predicted that it would take years for the general public to accept it.

Within a few months after its Paris opening, the film had been seen by 240,000 spectators, and by the beginning of 1961 the French version was establishing box-office records in every major city. Thus the public proved the snobs and many of the critics at Cannes wrong.

In an interview,[3] Antonioni summed up the plot of the film as follows:

"Superficially, *L'Avventura* may seem to be a love story, perhaps a somewhat mysterious one. During an excursion, a girl disappears. This fact creates a void which is immediately filled by other facts. For the fiancé and for one of the girl's friends, the search for her becomes a kind of sentimental journey, at the end of which they both find themselves in a new and quite unforeseen situation."

Everything in the film occurs as if its creator, in developing his theme, wished to deceive the spectator, to send him off on the wrong track the better to disconcert him. Relationships between the characters are established only to be modified as the story proceeds; events are presented not to advance the plot but to frustrate it. Antonioni defined his work a priori as "a mystery film in reverse." Thus, not only does the spectator never learn what has become of the girl who disappeared, but her father's dealings with the authorities, the results of the official inquest, the witnesses' suppositions, all vanish as well, like water into sand. This technique, if it were designed merely to create its own cunning effects, would be worthy of a Clouzot. But one would have to be unaware of Antonioni's seriousness to think that such a method could be

L'Avventura: Antonioni preparing a scene with Lea Massari and Gabriele Ferzetti.

L'Avventura: the final scene. Monica Vitti and Gabriele Ferzetti.

deliberately used by him against the audience, that it could constitute an end in itself.

According to age-old dramatic concepts, a story is constructed on a so-called logical foundation and centered on a logical sequence of events. In this light, *L'Avventura* is an illogical film. But what concerns Antonioni—and he has repeated this point often—is the characters and their behavior in relation to themselves and to events. Why, then, should he sustain our interest in facts that have ceased to interest the heroes of the story he is telling? The search for Anna, the court inquest, the consultation and interrogation of witnesses, are meaningful as long as they preoccupy the principal characters. When new facts take their place in the characters' minds, when new feelings are aroused, the earlier ones crumble away, lose all the reason they ever had for being dwelt upon. So, what at first glance seems disconcerting in *L'Avventura*, turns out, upon reflection, to derive from an unquestionably logical foundation. It is the new, not the traditional, method which is the true one.

It must, however, be pointed out that such a reversal justified the critical reservations of which we spoke earlier. The attention we are ordinarily required to pay to the "larger public" became, in this case, a danger, a danger to which we all more or less succumbed. What such a film requires of the spectator is no longer his *interest*, but his *availability*; he is required to integrate himself with the characters, to allow himself to be caught up in them, to live through their adventures, not as a stranger, especially not as a "spectator," but by a process of identification.

The majority of the critics were also unanimous in finding the film slow. "I should say thirty minutes too long," wrote Françoise Sagan, "but what do I know about such things?" Actually, this impression of slowness derives from the method we have just described. The audience is accustomed to concentrating on events and cannot easily enter into the characters. It is a habit, a deformity of our sensibilities, from which we cannot quickly free ourselves. See the film again, twice or three times, and the impression of slowness will disappear because, once we are familiar with the external incidents, the time, which once seemed empty because we were waiting to see what would happen next, becomes filled, is enriched, for thousands of reasons, and every image takes its proper place in a perfectly balanced construction.

Having said all this, we must add that, in spite of the considerable part played by women in it, *L'Avventura* is a masculine film. It deals with human relationships from the man's point of view. Sandro, the hero, is weak and pitiful (the reverse of Aldo), unsatisfied despite the satisfactions he mistakenly feels he permits himself, undeserving of the feelings he arouses and the events that center around him. But it is with him as a starting point and through him and around him that this strange ballet of separate solitudes is organized.

One further point has not been emphasized by critics as much as it deserves to be. This is the astonishing, subtle way in which Antonioni introduces his heroine into the story. The shy Claudia, passive at the beginning, acquires new life from scene to scene, achieving a dynamism which literally erases the image of the stubborn, sulky Anna and relegates her slowly to the condition in which the director wishes to place her: oblivion. This "revelation" of Claudia (using the word as one might refer to a photograph) provides a singular justification for Sandro's behavior as well as for her own. She is gradually transformed by the love that fills her. "Is it possible to change and forget in such a short time?" Claudia asks. The psychological substitution, going beyond the physical substitution of one woman for another, is what endows the plot with its full credibility. The evolution of Claudia, in contrast with Sandro's pitiful vacuity, is to go still further, to result in the final compromise in which once again it is she who takes the initiative, who offers the pity, the pardon, that her lover has not even had the courage to ask.

Thus an apparently ill-constructed story fits in with a bold new idea of drama. This idea demands not merely a new style but an entirely different form from that of traditional narrative. Most striking is the slowness of transition between external scenes, a slowness which is a direct result of the interdependence of the psychological processes taking place within the various characters. The story must be read through a lacework of images that are no longer to be regarded as acts, but as consequences of acts. The fact or the feeling or the character trait in question is not revealed to the spectator by the image; the process has been reversed. In this way, Antonioni also achieved a renovation—or, rather, an innovation—by opening up previously unsuspected horizons to the cinema. That the public, contrary to all expectations, should have accepted this new form and this new conception, both equally revolutionary, is the ultimate proof that they answered a definite need. *L'Avventura* is not only a beautiful film; it also marks the beginning of a new age.

We have emphasized earlier the unity of Antonioni's works. Within that unity the ideas behind his films meet, separate and reinforce each other while traveling along different paths. In contrast to *Il Grido*—the perfect symphony, self-enclosed, dense and rigorous—*L'Avventura* and *La Notte* open onto wide horizons, lengthen out, unfold like fans. In contrast to the fixity of the characters in *Il Grido,* the two later films present malleability, the "availability" of the couple in crisis. Had Antonioni's much discussed pessimism evolved into a more human sort of indulgence?

His lucidity remains complete; there is no more room for illusion than before—which is why so much interest attaches to the new escape route, the new "attitude," in which we can detect the emergence of a new consciousness, a desire to build on the ruins of the old dilemma. *Il Grido* touches the bottommost point of despair. Antonioni could have gone no further along that line without losing contact with humanity. He returns to the human plane in his next two films. He takes the first steps toward a reaction which can be read as no more than a fragile hope. For the acceptance of human weakness is the only evidence of any real force. Sandro and Claudia, Giovanni and Lidia, have deceived themselves about themselves. But with the new consciousness that they now possess they may be able to understand each other and love each other anew, more clear-sightedly; hence, more forcefully and with more validity. The director himself has advanced along the path he had laid out: to denounce illusion as a dangerous breeding ground for disintegration, to advance ever farther toward lucidity.

It does not seem necessary at this point to return to an examination of the psychological themes expressed in *L'Avventura*, and in *La Notte* (the second film stands as a kind of corollary to the first). The problem of the couple, the inability to communicate between human beings, the solitude of the soul torn between passions, instincts and feelings—all this has been very capably brought out by many critics. Antonioni himself has explained his ideas on various occasions, although he is always less concerned with making us accept the tragic evidence of his films than he is with urging us, once we have taken that evidence into account, to seek to revise our ways of understanding and feeling.

Nor is it useful to enter into a discussion of Antonioni's atheism or his interest in Marxism. While it can be argued that they explain his moral position, they certainly do not determine it. The same holds true for his work. "The man who tells a story," he once said, "is a human being, with his own points of view, his own opinions, his own sincerity. When I finished *L'Avventura*, I was forced to reflect on what it meant. . . ."[4] Just as we, the spectators, are forced to reflect.

Through the stories he uncovers, rather than imagines, the director brings forth his own experience as a human being and hands it over to us. Each spectator will see it and judge it according to what lies within him. The important thing is that the story open the debate by presenting the question with sincerity.

One privilege that Antonioni allows himself is that of lavishing attention on every character. His earlier films, particularly *Le Amiche*, were revealing in this regard. In *L'Avventura*, this particular quality gives the film an extra dimension. It is not only the images of Anna, Claudia and Sandro that are revealed to us. Each of the characters, no matter how episodic he may be—the old fisherman, the smuggler, the pair of druggists—has an extraordinary density. None is a mere walk-on, the plaything of a plot that lightly brushes him; each is a human being, true and total. Think of the way in which the passengers aboard the yacht appear on deck one after the other. They are sketched in with a few masterly strokes. Giulia, Corrado, Patrizia, Raimondo live side by side with the central trio, attend the drama, but without ever ceasing for a second to carry on their own mediocre pursuits, without ever giving up their own indolent self-regard. They give us an eloquent image—something like the main theme restated in a minor key —of each man's solitude amid the indifference of the many. Anna is quickly forgotten and left to her fate. What do the others do, even while pretending to participate in the search, but carry on with their own adventures? Giulia with her humiliation, Corrado with his scorn, Patrizia with her boredom. . . . It is this spectacle that first makes Claudia suffer, before she herself feels her friendship for the lost girl weaken under the glance that draws her to Sandro. Here the director demonstrates a mastery of technique. The comings and goings of his characters on the island are wed to the movements of the waves returning tirelessly to their attack on the bare rocks; the same vain activity exerted against the same unfeeling emptiness. There is a rising tide of restlessness, like the storm that looms up, in the consciousness that gradually comes over the characters that there has been a real, inexplicable disappearance. But this is more a threat than a fact. Claudia alone is shaken by it, yet her growing passion draws even her away from the object of her uneasiness and forces her to surrender in the same way as Sandro has done—to the selfishness of her feelings. This disturbs her all the more, builds up her hostility toward him, together with his growing attraction for her. The wide shots of rocks and sea, the characters pursuing their vain quest—this most "vacant" moment in the film is also the most gripping. For Sandro, the object of the search has already changed. On the very island where Anna has disappeared, it is now Claudia whom he seeks and who flees him through the long scenes interspersed with the indifferent actions of the others and the ridiculous efforts of police and frogmen to establish a dramatic conclusion. An entirely new psychological problem has already emerged and demands a solution. Once again, as in *Il Grido,* we find the interweaving of external events and interior drama.

It is surely in this expressive density that Antonioni's art has proved most powerful and most revolutionary. The scenes which appear at first glance most unnecessary always have a meaning, are always justified sooner or later in the film, and serve to enrich it. But they do not add up directly to a setting or mood; they do not take their places in a construction organized arbitrarily from without. Rather, they are inserted in a long succession of images that acquires significance from the cumulative effect of many small touches. To eliminate one or another would not topple the whole edifice but it would diminish the scope of the theme, would impoverish it.

L'Avventura has the breadth and complex structure of the novel, as well as its flexibility. Indeed, some critics have made comparisons between Proust and Antonioni, although the latter's style is the lighter and—dare I say?—the more subtle of the two. Another reason we think of the novel in relation to Antonioni's film lies in the contrast between these films and the theater-oriented cinema we have known for the past thirty years. The maker of *Il Grido* has surely "de-theatricalized" present-day cinema. It is this achievement which will give him a crucial position in the history of the Seventh Art.

But if we wish to find precedents for the new film form, why not seek them in the cinema itself? Antonioni's art seems to me to reach out over the past thirty years—during which dialogue has been the determining factor in film-making—and to join forces with the silent films, many of which attempted to deal with very complex themes. Exactly because dialogue no longer explains the action, as it has nearly always done in film since 1930, it has become in Antonioni's work an integral part of the whole, like the setting, characters or lighting.

Dialogue is related to another element: time. As in silent films (where explanatory titles were added, of course), Antonioni makes ellipses. He can also stretch time out. Thus the cinema regains the freedom it had lost, and the unfolding of action is no longer bound up with real time. The slowdown in rhythm which characterized the last few years of the silent film makes the family likeness even more obvious. *L'Avventura* is certainly closer to *The Fall of the House of Usher,* which was silent, than to *Carnival in Flanders.* In its efforts to express, rather than to say, the film of tomorrow will return to the wellsprings of an art which since the addition of the spoken word has followed too narrow a path.

6. *La Notte* and the Future

L'Avventura had yet to be seen outside Italy when Antonioni began work on another film. After the exception, *Il Grido*, the director had returned in *L'Avventura* to middle-class society. With *La Notte*, he also returned to a northern setting.

Milan, a feverishly growing octopus-like city with a tight grip on the men who inhabit it, breeds a constant desire to escape into some kind of freedom—whether through brutality, violence or madness. Beneath the drama of the couple, the major theme of the film, is a secondary drama: the city's inexorable grip on human beings. Antonioni's themes are never more linear than his story line; they cross, they complement one another. It is life, of course, but it is also perhaps the city which, over ten years, has killed the love that Antonioni dissects in *La Notte*. The action opens in late afternoon, continues through the sleepless night and closes in the dawn, a harrowing, gray dawn, just as *L'Avventura* does.

This night was to consume many weeks; this dawn was to take days rising. The single sequence of the party took thirty-two nights to shoot, from five in the evening until seven in the morning, at the Barlassina Country Club, which was transformed for the occasion into a villa. In the streets of Milan, in an elegant Milanese home, Antonioni shot a film with a plot even looser than that of *L'Avventura*. It revolves on a brief moment of the present, providing a sort of meditation on what no longer is, on what might have been and what may still be.

The film opens on a man in agony. Indeed, the film itself is one long portrait of agony. In an elegant hospital, a writer (Tommaso) still at the height of his powers is preparing to depart a life about which we know nothing except that it has not given him the love he desired. This love is Lidia, the wife of his friend Giovanni, a young novelist who has, unlike Tommaso, been given everything: love, health, fortune, success. In the course of the long day and night which follow, Lidia and Giovanni become aware of their disunity. Each in turn draws close to and then pulls away from the other. Giovanni comes to feel that all he once had is gone. At the party, a new personage looms up on his horizon: Valentina. She is the unknown, the possible. But in spite of her lucidity, she will also fail to cross the border of her own solitude. Giovanni attempts to revive his dead love for Lidia with physical desire—a hope even frailer than the one that guided Claudia's hand when she reached out to her lover's distress. On the golf course, the sun rises over the misty foliage like an ever-renewed promise traveling toward an often disappointed hope. Giovanni and Lidia attempt, in a more secret way now, to know one another—to join their separate solitudes.

With the slow exposition of a relationship revealed during a single day, the author mingles several quests: that of Lidia, searching for memories that can do nothing but confirm the death of her love; that of Valentina, sickened in advance by the life that awaits her; that of Giovanni, who does not know where to concentrate his desires, where to find a shred of hope. We are presented with a multiple progression, like life itself, perpetually reborn out of its own death.

"Michelangelo Antonioni is the film maker of the inner life," Claude Mauriac wrote.[1] "Out of its difficulties he makes difficult films; out of its weaknesses, he creates strong works. *La Notte* restates the fundamental theme of *L'Avventura*, suggesting in images and words that which can neither be seen nor expressed: the invisible, the indescribable and yet perceptible conclusion of a love. Or rather, its impalpable crumbling. The novelty lies in the fact that he does not present an ephemeral love affair but a marriage which has lasted into its tenth year. In the death of their jealousy, the couple recognize the death of their love. In addition, we have a second theme which was indicated retrospectively in *L'Avventura* but is here examined directly: the sacrifice of art to money."

Giovanni surrenders, like Sandro, to the pressure for financial security. This surrender is a theme equally dear and bitter to Antonioni. It represents still another defeat, and a no less distressing one than the defeat of love.

L'Avventura, a drama of human solitude, was set in the loneliness of an empty island; *La Notte*, the drama of men imprisoned in themselves, is set within the architectural prison that the city

La Notte:
"Lidia (Jeanne Moreau) as a tiny figure at the foot of a wall which seems about to crush her..."

"...she is a prisoner..."

builds around us. The setting once again constitutes more than a mere backdrop; it synthesizes—even more than it symbolizes—the inner drama. And it is itself the condition of that drama.

It therefore seems to me nonsensical to complain, as several critics have, that there is a too obvious straining after formal effects in *La Notte*. The fact that Lidia is shown to us as a tiny figure at the foot of a wall which seems about to crush her; that the lines of the interior settings follow the rigorous style of "functional" architecture which, originally built to serve man, now circumvents him; that most of the camera angles emphasize this same subservience of man to his environment—there is no gratuitous formalism in any of this, nor mere symbolism. All is a response to the real demands of a form of expression which does not limit itself to precise explanations of dialogue or to the plasticity of the human face. Antonioni studies the relationships between people, but he also seeks to make clearer the relationships between the individual and his surroundings. His art is, as was said before, an antidramatic art—by which I mean that it lies beyond dramatic convention; a cosmic art, calling into play all the elements of which it is composed.

The subsidiary episodes in *La Notte*, like those in *Il Grido*, contribute significantly to the exploration of the central theme. What Lidia is searching for as she wanders along the outskirts of Milan is not only, nor even especially, memories of her love. She is fleeing the implacable condition of everything that binds her: the geometry of the buildings, the smooth house fronts, the rigidly channeled flood of automobiles, the swarming crowds; she is trying to regain, amid the disorder of vacant lots and crumbling walls and human misery, something alive, something magical and vague. She makes contact once again with life in the raw, with the violence of young boys, the open desire of the men she passes; she creates for herself the illusion of escaping from the net which holds her prisoner. For she is a prisoner, like the guests at the villa moving in circles about the green lawns, meeting, taking stock of one another, all prisoners of the same condition from which they now attempt to escape, in their nocturnal follies, to the slow rhythms of a joyless orchestra. The individual theme overflows and is "superimposed" on the collective. At dawn, nothing

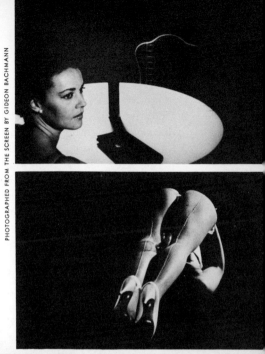

La Notte: the night-club sequence. Jeanne Moreau as Lidia.

remains but the bitterness, the futility, of beginning again. Neither love nor freedom will be reborn. Beyond the park and its foliage, the city is about to reawaken and to set into motion again the agonies of the night.

As in *L'Avventura,* Antonioni rejects traditional dramatic construction. He does not even make the pretense of constructing a story, but chooses several themes which he intermingles, following their apparently disordered progress along with us, brushing against various faces, various destinies, abandoning them, opening his film in the unknown territory of the past (Tommaso's as well as the couple's) only to close on the equally unknown ground of the future.

While reducing the *time* of what one can hardly describe as the "action," he stretches it out to great lengths in the *expression,* constructing his film from broad sequences, their length based on their duration in real life. The moments of the night are experienced in their totality, sometimes even—as in the night-club scene with the Negro dancer—to the point of tiresome insistence, intended to draw us into the characters' own boredom.

We see here a sort of Proustian desire to make us enter the psychological world of the characters. It is an imperious desire. Does it not present a real danger, that of once again drawing the cinema out of its proper domain? Is it not possible that this new approach, making use of all the techniques of the novel, may create a literary cinema which will soon prove as vain as the theatrical cinema it is meant to replace?

La Notte moves beyond the horizons opened up by *L'Avventura,* but in doing so it sometimes falsifies them. "I believe it is much more cinematographic to try to catch a character's thoughts by showing his reactions, whatever they may be, rather than by wrapping the whole thing up in a speech, an explanation."[2] *La Notte* runs the risk of denying this insight, expressed by Antonioni himself in 1957. The inner progression of the characters' thoughts is indeed expressed by outward behavior and action, but, all the same, the film closes with an "explanation"—the dialogue between Giovanni and Lidia on the golf course at dawn. Here the writer in Antonioni wins out over the director. The emergence of a less subtle film form lies at the end of this line of development. For what wins us in Antonioni's art is the reticence which not only causes him to avoid cheap emotional effects but even prevents him from saying all he could say. His is an art based on shades of meaning, but still more on things left unsaid, on secrets—an art that does not easily reveal itself, that forces us to discover it.

Although there is perhaps more dialogue in *L'Avventura*, it is not a literary film because it has a meaning apart from that dialogue. It is difficult to say as much for *La Notte*. Thus there are more differences than similarities between the two works. This point brings us to another problem which should be mentioned at least parenthetically: that of the dubbing. Not only Jeanne Moreau's lines but all dialogue was dubbed, with different voices from those of the actors, in the original Italian version of *La Notte*. Antonioni copies too closely from life for us not to be somewhat disturbed by the results of this. Even though the dubbing was personally supervised by him, the film still lost something in authenticity.

Critics have pointed out other weaknesses in *La Notte*. Some of these seem to me irrelevant; for example, the comparison between *La Notte* and *La Dolce Vita*, particularly with respect to the all-night party. Because the two films are of the same period, because they deal with the same problems and depict the same social environment, it is inevitable that resemblances should be found between Antonioni and Fellini. But these are more apparent than real. What is so striking in *La Notte* is that, even more than in *L'Avventura*, the director refuses to indulge the audience in any way at all. He presents his characters as if reflecting them in a mirror—a mirror incapable even for an instant of flattering them, of surprising them in a gesture that might show them to us otherwise than as they are in the depths of their beings. From this comes their absolute truthfulness. In *La Notte*, Antonioni describes even less of an "adventure." On the contrary, we have here something like the climax of a long, slowly developed plot which, day by day, year by year, has led its protagonists closer to their moment of self-awareness. And if, in order to express this, the director has taken great care with his camera angles and worked out a sophisticated interpretation of his setting and theme, still there is great simplicity; there is purity in the gray photography, in the total absence of music apart from that belonging to actual happenings on the screen, in the purposely "toneless" interplay between man and wife.

The ultimate reservation we ought to feel with regard to *La Notte* seems to me to rest on quite different ground. That reservation concerns the society which the film depicts.

"I prefer to set my heroes in a rich environment because then their feelings are not (as among the poorer classes) determined by material and practical contingencies." These lines, written by Antonioni about *L'Avventura*, apply equally to *La Notte*. It is this very freedom from "material and practical contingencies" which troubles us. The man who is deprived of material struggle turns in on himself, questions himself, and the resulting vacuity deforms his feelings, creating problems which often could not exist except as a function of his material or social freedom. In most of Antonioni's films, the characters are indeed less interesting than their feelings. There is a danger, then, that we may be led little by little into a kind of pointless intellectual game, because these feelings—these problems—have been falsified. In its day, neorealism saved the Italian cinema by making it aware of external reality; it plunged man into his own environment, his own era. Will we be forced to turn "the problem of the bicycle," of which Antonioni himself has spoken (see p. 90), into an argument against him?

The author's intention is, of course, none other than to demonstrate the vanity of bourgeois society, but, as a direct consequence and at the same time, he demonstrates the emptiness of the feelings that occur within it. The sentimental complexes of these couples with their love-sickness will become as foreign to us and as useless as the consuming passions of the divas of the Gay Nineties. Here, then, is the danger to be glimpsed within *La Notte*. The superimposed negations cancel one another out. Any human problem detached from its social or cosmic context becomes nothing more than a mere intellectual exercise.

If *Il Grido* attains a kind of grandeur, this is precisely because its characters live, suffer, fight, are forced to face facts. They are men and women, not merely case studies in amorous or intellectual psychology. They do more than interest us; they move us. Antonioni's later films, like their characters, run the risk of becoming limited to their own elegant negations, of turning into nothing more than an aspect of the very vanity they denounce. It is reported[3] that Antonioni, during a visit to the studio of the painter Mark Rothko, told him, "Your paintings are like my films—about nothing, with precision"—a statement which could define a whole new art or lead to a dead end.

But can such a danger exist for a creator whose strongest characteristic is the refusal to accept stagnation? Whose desire is to advance ever further as an artist, not to "renew himself"—for such a wish can be felt only by the second-rate—but to *advance*, along what path and by what means he does not himself yet know? People say that Antonioni is a *modern* director; if true, it is in this sense of wanting always to advance. He fears neither risks nor contradictions, whether they arise in the substance or in the form of his work, if they contribute to his requirements for expression. After refusing to use the action-reaction (or reverse camera angle) shooting technique at the beginning of his career, he returned to it later; after almost entirely doing away with foreground (in *Il Grido*), he alternated broad, long shots with extreme close-ups in *L'Avventura*, scanning faces with an unparalleled keenness of vision. After depicting Aldo's erotic adventures with an almost old-fashioned restraint, he treated the amorous frolics of Sandro and his mistress with a truly modern insistence, following in the footsteps of Ingmar Bergman.

On this point, we might add a further observation. It is indeed true that the scene between Sandro and Claudia by the railroad track is an "admirable love song"—to use one critic's phrase. Antonioni's distinctive style, when it is applied to scenes of this kind, transforms the act of love into a kind of poem—a lyric poem in *L'Avventura*, a tragic, even grotesque, poem in the sequence of the nymphomaniac in *La Notte*. Again there is a danger: that this kind of transmutation of effect, based on the sheer genius of the author, may create still another stereotype, which will quickly become unbearable. Such scenes, in spite of their plastic and lyrical qualities, strike me as immodest, not because of their erotic nature but for the same reasons that the grief-ravaged faces in which the cinema once gloried today seem indecent. Suffering, like pleasure, should be suggested, not detailed. The evolution of the cinema has brought with it new techniques for expressing pain which are all the more moving for being quieter. The expression of sensual pleasure has still to find a parallel course, has still to develop more appropriate techniques for achieving a similar eloquence.

It is pointless to attack individual details of Antonioni's art. Despite his maturity, his mastery, he does not feel that he has "arrived." In his interviews, he carefully avoids being trapped in any system, in setting limits or establishing rules for his art. Speaking about certain aspects of his work on which a critic had commented, Antonioni said recently: "Perhaps that is true about the films I have made up till now; it will no longer be true in the films I am going to make from now on. We change continually; our interests change. Who can say what we will do tomorrow? For myself, I don't know. . . ."

And this is doubtless the reason he attaches so little importance to what are called the influences of his youth; or rather, why he sees in them nothing more than assimilated material, out of which the present is built, but from which—for the very reason that they *have* been assimilated—he is now detached. This concern for the present also explains why the director is so exclusively interested in the problems of the couple, in the reactions of adults. There is no place for the child, nor for the old man, in his universe. On this point, it is revealing to note that one crucial problem, the problem of the child, is not even taken into account in the treatment of a couple like the one in *La Notte*. But we may expect that Antonioni will eventually broaden the types of human relationships presented in his films.

His essential desire is to remain "available," open to the future. In his own life, it appears that this is the case: "I have no country house. I own no land, I do what it suits me to do at any given moment."

In this concern with living, the work that he has chosen to do holds a primary position, for it reflects his thoughts and his preoccupations. As is true of all highly creative people, his art is less a planned body of work than a direct and necessary expression of his ideas and his passions. This is what gives it its value. At the heart of Antonioni's films we find something more than the previously unknown resources of an art form; we find the conscience of a man.

II

ANTONIONI ON THE CINEMA

●

Art and Man

[Reply to a questionnaire on neorealism, originally published in *Bianco e Nero*, September 1958; republished in different form as part of "Fare un film e per me vivere" in *Cinema Nuovo*, March–April 1959]

Making a film is not like writing a book. Flaubert said that living was not his trade; his trade was writing. Making a film, however, *is* living; at least it is for me. (I draw this flattering comparison, of course, only to give some tone to my remarks.) My personal life is not interrupted during the shooting of a film; indeed, it is then that it becomes most intense. What is one's compulsion to pour all the wine of one's personal life into the cask of the film, if not a way of participating in life, of adding something worthwhile (or at least intended to be so) from one's personal heritage—the richness or the poverty of which it is up to others to assess?

Since a film is a public spectacle, it is obvious that one's own affairs cease to be private, and they too become public property. For my own part, today, I have a clearly defined feeling on this subject (by today I mean in this postwar period, so full of disturbing facts, so thick with anxieties and fears about the destiny of the whole world). It is my feeling that to go on ignoring certain subjects is a distinct error, precisely because we are men of the cinema and thus exposed to the public view. We no longer have the right to allow it to be believed that our private lives continue as they once did. I should like to borrow a quotation from Giraudoux that I read in a newspaper article: "There are moments when one does not speak of trees, because one is angry with trees." And indeed, the least worthy thing an intellectual can do when faced with the grave events that trouble the world is to go on concerning himself with subjects that distract attention from the seriousness of those events. . . .

No one talked of neorealism during the war, nor even during the period immediately after the war. Searing reality gave birth to a movement which the critics later christened "neorealism." I believe that we are today, *mutatis mutandis,* living in an identical climate. I do not know what sort of films we will be able to make, but I want to find out. I feel that there is one thing that we absolutely must do: defend the principle of intelligence within the heart of the real. And reject the mental laziness and conformity of the many.

I know that by speaking in this way I lay myself open to the accusation of alarmism. It is a fashionable kind of accusation. It is also true that in Italy, where public opinion is nonexistent, no one in recent times has been afraid of war. It is also true that in France the most amazing sort of resignation has prevailed, despite the high intellectual level of that nation. But these are, at most, arguments in my favor. In any case, there is more than simply a moral commitment behind my remarks. I think that we men of the cinema must always find inspiration in our own era. Not so much to express and interpret it in its harshest and most tragic aspects, as to pick up from it the echoes it produces within us so that we, men of the cinema, may be sincere and coherent within ourselves, and honest and courageous with others. This is the one and only way to be alive. Intelligence which evades its responsibilities at a given moment is a contradiction in terms.

●　　●　　●

[Fabio Rinaudo, "Foyer-Antonioni," *Croniche del Cinema e della Televisione,* No. 7, December 1955]

Dear Rinaudo, you ask me what I want to do in the cinema, or what I want to say, or what I want to be. I thought I could answer you. And yet, on the contrary, I have been sitting here in front of my typewriter for a half hour now, and every time I strike the keys and form a word, I feel as if I were playing a role. That is just it. Playing a role I have not learned. It is not only unattractive to talk about oneself, it is difficult as well. Then, perhaps it is entirely impossible to foresee the ideas and the impulses we will have in the future, and the experiments we will make. We live so tightly bound up in reality, and reality changes so quickly. The *turris eburnea* has crumbled away. The greatest effort is the effort to be oneself. That is to say, to make films which have some meaning in one's personal life, without straying into the confessional. This is the only way they can have meaning for others. You have asked me, after all, to state a poetic theory. And I answer that if I were sufficiently sure of being an artist to give a reply, then I should have closed myself off forever from the possibility of truly becoming one some day.

• • •

[Enrico Roda, "37 Domande a Michelangelo Antonioni," *Tempo*, Milan, July 4, 1957]

Q: What is the problem that lies closest to your heart?
A: Can there exist a saint without God?
Q: In a world without film, what would you have made?
A: Film.
Q: To what do you attribute your present activity?
A: To film.
Q: What do you feel is your principle fault, as a man?
A: Modesty.
Q: And as an artist?
A: It takes courage to write: "As an artist, I feel that . . ." Courage I don't have.

The Author and His Theme

["Entretien," *Cahiers du Cinéma*, October 1960]

The principle behind the cinema, like that behind all the other arts, rests on a choice. It is, in Camus' words, "the revolt of the artist against the real."

If one holds to this principle, what difference can it make by what means reality is revealed? Whether the author of a film seizes on the real in a novel, in a newspaper story or in his own imagination, what counts is the way he isolates it, stylizes it, makes it his own. The plot of *Crime and Punishment,* apart from the form given it by Dostoyevsky, is a perfectly ordinary plot. One could make a very beautiful or a very ugly film out of it. This is why I have nearly always written original stories for my films. Once it happened that I fell in love at first sight with a novella by Pavese. While working on it I realized that I liked it for quite different reasons from those which had made me think of it for the film. And the pages that had interested me most were those that lent themselves least to film adaptation. Then again, it is very difficult to get one's bearings in someone else's story, for the raw materials are chosen with reference to the style of a story that one has clearly in mind. So, in the long run, I find it much simpler to invent the story out of whole cloth. A director is a man, therefore he has ideas; he is also an artist, therefore he has imagination. Whether they are good or bad, it seems to me that I have an abundance of stories to tell. And the things I see, the things that happen to me, continually renew the supply.

•   •   •

["Questions à Antonioni," *Positif,* July 1959]

. . . Reality changes so rapidly that if one theme is not dealt with, another presents itself. Allowing one's attention to be attracted by each little thing has become a vice of the imagination. All one has to do is to keep one's eyes open: everything becomes full of meaning; everything cries out to be interpreted, reproduced. Thus, there is no one particular film that I would like to make; there is one for every single theme I perceive. And I am excited by these themes, day and night. However, opportunity and other practical considerations limit and direct the choice. . . .

I never begin with an idea in order to end with a story. The majority of the stories that have taken form in my hands have come from outside, from germs which I have, as it were, breathed from the air. It can happen that films acquire meanings, that is to say, the meanings appear afterwards, which is natural enough. I am a man, and, of course, I am not without my own opinions. I do wish to say that suicide is not one of my preoccupations; it is only one among the very many possible solutions to the problem of life. A dreary solution, certainly, but as legitimate as any other. If life is a gift, then so must be the freedom we have to deprive ourselves of it.

•   •   •

["Colloquo con Michelangelo Antonioni," *Bianco e Nero,* June 1958]

. . . It is obvious, and this is a general truth, that everything which has happened to me in life has impelled me to create certain stories rather than certain others. That much I can say with confidence, but it is impossible for me to give an exact account of the cinematographic or extra-cinematographic experiences that have contributed to my development. It is difficult to say how a story is born, how I got the ideas for *Cronaca di un Amore* and *Il Grido.* Films are born in me like poems in the heart of a poet (I do not mean to pass for a poet, I am only making a comparison). Words, images, concepts force themselves onto the mind, they are all mixed together, and the end result is a poem. And so it is, I believe, with films. Everything we read, feel, think and see takes on concrete form in images at a given moment, and from these images the story is born.

It is often real incidents that suggest stories, but this has happened to me only rarely—in fact just once, with *I Vinti.*

. . . I could not really say whether I am a neorealistic director. It is not true that neorealism is finished; it is evolving. A movement, an intellectual current, is never finished so long as it has not been replaced by a later development. There is never a gap in the continuity.

The neorealism of the postwar period, when reality itself was so searing and immediate, attracted attention to the relationship existing between the character and surrounding reality. It was precisely this relationship which was important and which created an appropriate cinema. Now, however, when for better or for worse reality has been normalized once again, it seems to me more interesting to examine what remains in the characters from their past experiences.

This is why it no longer seems to me important to make a film about a man who has had his bicycle stolen. That is to say, about a man whose importance resides (primarily and exclusively) in the fact that he has had his bicycle stolen. We do not seek to find out whether he is timid, whether he loves his wife, whether he is jealous, etc. We are not interested in these aspects of his character, because the only thing that counts is the theft of the bicycle which prevents him from working, and so we must follow the man on his search.

Now that we have eliminated the problem of the bicycle (I am speaking metaphorically), it is important to see what there is in the mind and in the heart of this man who has had his bicycle stolen, how he has adapted himself, what remains in him of his past experiences, of the war, of the period after the war, of everything that has happened to him in our country—a country which, like so many others, has emerged from an important and grave adventure.

Ideas and Facts

[This statement was distributed at Cannes when *L'Avventura* was presented there.]

There exists in the world today a very serious break between science on the one hand, always projecting into the future and each day ready to deny what it was the day before, if that will enable it to advance its conquest of the future even by a fraction. . . . between science on the one hand and a fixed, stiff morality on the other, the faults of which are perfectly apparent to man, but which still continues to stand.

From the moment he is born, man is burdened with a heavy

load of feelings. I do not say these feelings are old or out of date, but they are entirely unsuited to his needs; they condition him without aiding him, fetter him without ever showing him a way out of his difficulties.

And yet man has not succeeded—so it seems—in unburdening himself of this inheritance. He acts, he hates, he suffers, impelled by moral forces and myths which were already old in the time of Homer. Which is an absurdity in our day, on the eve of man's first journey to the moon. But that is the way things are!

Man, then, is ready to unburden himself of his technical or scientific knowledge when it proves false. Never before has science been so humble, so ready to retract its statements. But in the realm of the emotions, a total conformity reigns.

During the last few years, we have examined, studied the emotions as much as possible, to the point of exhaustion. This is all we have been able to do. But we have not been able to find any new emotions, nor even to get an inkling of a solution to the problem.

I do not pretend to be able, nor would it be possible for me, to find the solution. I am not a moralist.

My film L'Avventura is neither a denunciation nor a sermon. It is a story told in images, and I hope people will be able to see in it not the birth of a delusory emotion but the method by which it is possible to delude oneself in one's feelings. For, I repeat, we make use of an aging morality, of outworn myths, of ancient conventions. And we do this in full consciousness of what we are doing. Why do we respect such a morality?

The conclusion which my characters reach is not that of moral anarchy. They arrive, at best, at a sort of reciprocal pity. That too, you will tell me, is old. But what else is there left to us?

For example, what do you think this eroticism that has invaded literature and the performing arts really is? It is a symptom, and perhaps the easiest symptom to discern, of the illness from which the emotions are suffering.

We would not be erotic, that is, the sick men of Eros, if Eros himself were in good health. And when I say in good health, I mean just that: adequate to man's condition and needs.

Thus, there is discomfort. And, as always happens when he feels discomfort, man reacts; but he reacts badly, and he is unhappy about it.

In *L'Avventura,* the catastrophe is an erotic impulse of this order: cheap, useless, unfortunate. And it is not enough to know that this is the way things are. For the hero (what a ridiculous word!) of my film is perfectly aware of the crude nature, the uselessness, of the erotic impulse that gets the better of him. But this is not enough.

Here then is another fallen myth, the illusion that it is enough to *know oneself,* to analyze oneself minutely in the most secret places of the soul.

No, that is not enough. Each day we live through an "adventure," whether it be a sentimental, a moral or an ideological one.

But if we know that the old tables of the law no longer offer anything but words too often read out and repeated, why do we remain faithful to those tables? There is a stubbornness here that strikes me as pathetic.

Man, who has no fear of the scientific unknown, is frightened by the moral unknown.

If you have an enemy, do not try to beat him up, do not insult him, do not curse him, do not humiliate him, do not hope that he will have an automobile accident. Wish, quite simply, that he may remain without work. That is the most terrible hardship by which a man can be struck. Any vacation, even the most marvelous of vacations, has meaning only if it forms a counterweight to one's fatigue.

I consider that I am especially privileged in this matter—I do work that I enoy. I do not know many Italians who can say as much.

That work is the most important thing in my life. It would be superfluous to ask what it gives me. It gives me everything. It gives me the possibility to express myself, to communicate with others. Considering the difficulty I have in speaking, I would feel as if I were nonexistent without the cinema.

Directing

["Entretien," *Cahiers du Cinéma*, October 1960]

I am not a theoretician of the cinema. If you ask me what directing is, the first answer that comes into my head is: I don't know. The second: All my opinions on the subject are in my films. Among other things, I am an opponent of any separation of the various phases of the work. Such separation has an exclusively practical value. It is valuable for all those who participate in the work— except for the director, if he happens to be both author and director at once. To speak of directing as one of the phases in this work is to engage in a theoretical discussion which seems to me opposed to that unity of the whole to which every artist is committed during his work. Isn't it during the shooting that the final version of the scenario is arrived at? And, during the shooting, isn't everything automatically brought into question—from the theme to the dialogue itself, the real merit of which is never revealed until it is heard in the mouths of the actors?

Of course the moment always comes when, having collected one's ideas, certain images, an intuition of a certain kind of development—whether psychological or material—one must pass on to the actual realization. In the cinema, as in the other arts, this is the most delicate moment—the moment when the poet or writer makes his first mark on the page, the painter on his canvas, when the director arranges his characters in their setting, makes them speak and move, establishes, through the composition of his various images, a reciprocal relationship between persons and things, between the rhythm of the dialogue and that of the whole sequence, makes the movement of the camera fit in with the psychological situation. But the most crucial moment of all comes when the director gathers from all the people and from everything around him every possible suggestion, in order that his work may acquire a more spontaneous cast, may become more personal and, we might even say—in the broadest sense—more autobiographical. . . .

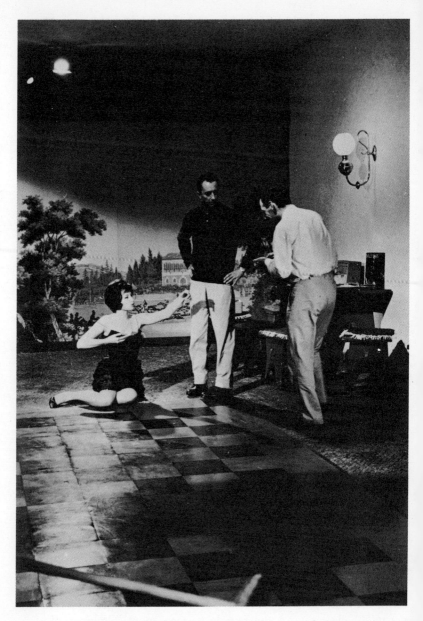

La Notte: Antonioni preparing a scene with Monica Vitti as Valentina.

Each stage in the creation of a film is of equal importance. It is not true that it is possible to establish a clear distinction between them. They all enter into the final synthesis. Thus it may happen that, during the working-out of the theme, a particular kind of shot might be decided upon—a traveling shot, for example; during the shooting, a character or a situation might be changed; or during the dubbing, one or more speeches might even be altered. For me, from the moment when the first, still unformed, idea comes into my head until the projection of the rushes, the process of making a film constitutes a single piece of work. I mean that I cannot become interested in anything, day or night, which is not that film. Let no one imagine that this is a romantic pose—on the contrary. I become relatively more lucid, more attentive, and almost feel as if I were more intelligent and more ready to understand. . . .

No one can fail to see that the shooting script has become less detailed than it was formerly, less detailed even than it was a few years ago. The technical directions have almost entirely disappeared, along with the right-hand column, the dialogue. In my own scripts, I have got to the point of leaving out the numbers by which we used to indicate each scene. (The script girl is the only person who uses them, because they facilitate her work.) And this, because it seems to me more logical to divide the scenes at the same time as you shoot them. Here we already have a way of improvising.

But there are others. I rarely feel the desire to reread a scene the day before the shooting. Sometimes I arrive at the place where the work is to be done and I do not even know what I am going to shoot. This is the system I prefer: to arrive at the moment when shooting is about to begin, absolutely unprepared, virgin. I often ask to be left alone on the spot for fifteen minutes or half an hour and I let my thoughts wander freely. I keep myself from doing anything but looking. I am helped by the things that surround me; they always give me suggestions. I have great sympathy with things, perhaps even more than with people, though it is the latter that interest me more.

In any case, I find that it is very useful to look over the location and to feel out the atmosphere while waiting for the actors. It may happen that the images before my eyes coincide with those I had in my mind, but this is not frequently the case. It more often happens that there is something insincere or artificial about the image one has thought of. Here again is another way of improvising.

But this is not all. It also sometimes happens that in trying out a scene I abruptly change my mind. Or that I change it gradually, as the camera crew sets up the lights and as I watch the actors move and speak under the arcs. In my opinion, it is only then that one can make a proper judgment of a scene and correct it.

•   •   •

["Colloquo con Michelangelo Antonioni," *Bianco e Nero*, June 1958]

The technique I use (which is an instinctive one, for I do not decide a priori to shoot in any given way) seems to me to be directly tied up with my desire to follow the characters in order to unveil their most hidden thoughts. I may perhaps be deceiving myself in thinking that one can make them speak by following them with the camera. But I believe it is much more cinematographic to try to catch a character's thoughts by showing his reactions, whatever they may be, than to wrap the whole thing up in a speech, than to resort to what practically amounts to an explanation.

One of my preoccupations when I am shooting is that of following the character until I feel the need to let him go . . . I follow him not because of any theoretical notion, but because it seems to me important to catch those of the character's thoughts which appear—but are not at all—the least significant.

When everything has been said, when the scene appears to be finished, there is what comes afterwards. It seems to me important to show the character, back and front, just at that moment—a gesture or an attitude that illuminates all that has happened, and what results from it.

It is in this spirit that I try to shoot the scenes of my films. I do not read what I am about to shoot each morning—I know the scenario by heart; thus I do not need to study it every morning at my desk. When I arrive at the studio, I ask everyone to leave for a quarter of an hour or twenty minutes, the time required to try out the camera movements, to soak myself in them, to run through the sequence from a technical point of view. I do not shoot several times over, I do not change, I have no doubts about the position of the camera. Obviously, these are problems I set myself, but I resolve them at the beginning and then do not change afterwards.

Naturally I cannot work out camera movements at my desk, I have to think about them at the studio. . . . I always use a dolly, even when I am going to shoot an important scene (besides, I prefer vertical rather than horizontal movements). I follow the characters with the movements I have already worked out, and I correct them later if need be. I compose my scenes from behind the camera. Certain directors—for instance, René Clair—work in a different way. I do not say that theirs is not a legitimate system, but I cannot understand how they manage to shoot from little designs and plans they have drawn on paper ahead of time. I feel that the composition is a plastic, figurative element which ought to be seen in its exact dimensions.

The Elements of the Film

[*L'Express*, September 8, 1960]

Q: Why do you use only natural settings?

A: Because they stimulate me more. It is the same as it might be with a painter to whom someone said, "Here is a wall which is to be covered with frescoes, so many yards long and so many yards high." These are the kinds of limitations which aid rather than fetter the imagination.

Q: Sometimes you transform your natural setting, you give it an appearance it does not actually possess, you work over it, you select it . . .

A: Yes, that's true. But you are describing a temptation I have every time I go anywhere, to an office or to a private home. Some-

"I compose my scenes from behind the camera." During the production of *L'Eclisse*. Below, with Monica Vitti.

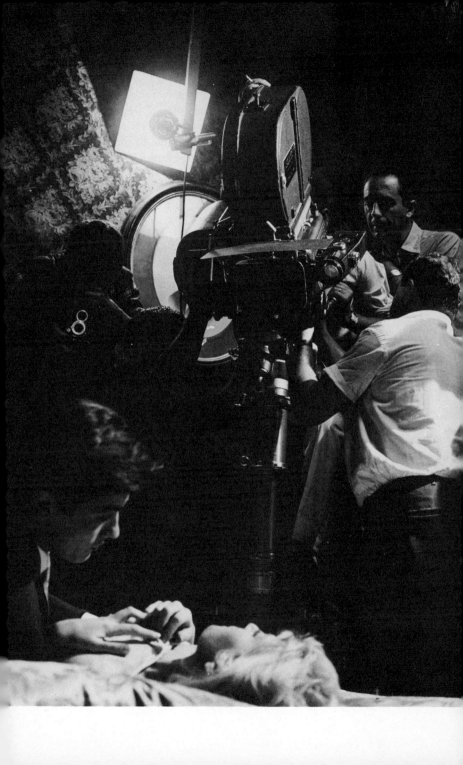

times it even arises in my own house. Someone comes to see me and suddenly, during the conversation, I begin to feel uneasy; it is because I feel that we are badly placed in the room, we are badly seated. He is on a sofa, I am next to him, while I ought to be seated opposite him. And instead of a wall with a picture on it behind the back of the man I am speaking to, I should like to have a window, perhaps even so that I could distract myself by looking out. When I shoot a film, that is all I am doing. I arrange things and people the way they ought to be.

• • •

["Entretien," *Cahiers du Cinéma,* October 1960]

I attribute enormous importance to the sound track, and I always try to take the greatest care with it. And when I say the sound track, I am talking about the natural sounds, the background noises rather than the music. For *L'Avventura,* I had an enormous number of sound effects recorded: every possible quality of the sea, more and less stormy, the breakers, the rumble of the waves in the grottoes. I had a hundred reels of tape filled with nothing but sound effects. Then I selected those that you hear on the film's sound track. For me, that is the true music, the music that can be adapted to images. Conventional music only rarely melts into the image; more often it does nothing but put the spectator to sleep, and it prevents him from appreciating what he is seeing. After long consideration, I am relatively opposed to "musical commentary," at least in its present form. I detect something old and rancid in it. The ideal solution would be to create a sound track out of noises and to call on an orchestra leader to conduct it. But then, wouldn't the only orchestra leader capable of doing that be the director himself?

The Actor

[*L'Express*, February 28, 1961]

The film actor ought not to *understand*, he ought to *be*. One might argue that in order to be, he needs to understand. This is not true. If it were true, the most intelligent actor would be the best actor. Reality often proves the contrary.

When an actor is intelligent, the effort he has to make to be a good actor is three times as great, for he wants to get to the bottom of everything, even the finest shades of meaning, and in trying to do so he trespasses on ground that is not his own—in fact, he creates obstacles for himself.

His reflections on the character he is playing, which, according to popular theory, should lead him to an exact characterization, end by hamstringing his work and depriving him of naturalness. The actor should arrive on the set in a virgin state. The more intuitive his work, the more spontaneous it will be.

The actor ought not to work on the psychological level but on the level of the imagination. And the imagination is lit up spontaneously; it has no electric buttons to press.

It is not possible to have true collaboration between actor and director. They work on two quite different levels. The director owes the actor no explanations except general ones about the character and the film. It is dangerous to go into details. Sometimes the actor and the director necessarily become enemies. The director must not compromise himself by revealing his intentions. The actor is a kind of Trojan horse within the director's citadel.

My favorite method consists in bringing about certain results by a certain amount of secret labor. I mean, by stimulating the actor to realize possibilities which lie in him but of whose existence he is himself unaware; by exciting not his intelligence but his instinct; by giving him not justifications but illuminations. One may even go so far as to cheat with the actor: to ask him for one thing in order to obtain another. The director ought to know how to discern and to separate the good and the bad, the useful and the superfluous, in what the actor has to offer.

The most important quality in a director is the ability to see. It is also valuable in directing actors. The actor is one of the elements in the image. A modification of his pose or gesture modifies the image itself. A speech which the actor makes in profile gives a different weight from one spoken full-face. A speech made with the camera placed overhead has a different value from a speech made with the camera below.

These are only a few very simple observations, but they prove what the director is: the man who composes the scene, who has to decide upon and then judge the actor's pose, gestures and movements.

The same is true for the speaking of the dialogue. The voice is one "noise" mingled with other noises, and the relationship among them is fully understood only by the director. Thus it is up to him to establish the balance, or imbalance, between various noises.

One has to listen to an actor for a long time, even when he is merely making mistakes. One has to allow him his mistakes and still try to understand how it may be possible to use his errors in the film; for his errors are, at that particular moment, the most spontaneous thing he has to offer.

To explain a scene or a piece of dialogue is to treat all the actors in the same way, for the scene and the dialogue do not change. All actors, however, require special treatment. Hence the need to seek out other methods. In short, the problem consists in leading the actor little by little into the right path, by means of apparently innocent corrections which must never arouse his suspicions.

This method of working may seem paradoxical, but it is the only one that enables the director to obtain a satisfactory result with amateur actors, actors whom, as we say, we "pick up off the streets." Neorealism taught us this. But it is also applicable to professional actors, even to the greatest among them.

I wonder whether there exists a really great film actor; what a great film actor would be like. The actor who thinks too much is troubled by one ambition: to be great. This is a terrible obstacle, and it carries with it the risk that his playing may be deprived of much of its truthfulness.

I do not *think* I have two legs. I *have* them. If the actor seeks to understand, he thinks. If he thinks, it will be difficult for him to

Betsy Blair
as Elvia
in *Il Grido*.

Monica Vitti
as she appears
in *L'Eclisse*.

find the power to be humble. And humility constitutes the best single point of departure in any attempt to find the truth.

Sometimes an actor is intelligent enough to overcome his limitations and discover for himself the proper path to follow—that is, he uses his own intelligence in order to apply the method I have described.

When this happens, the actor has the qualities of a director.

•   •   •

["Colloquo con Michelangelo Antonioni," *Bianco e Nero*, June 1958]

The problem that arises most often for a director is that of creating a harmonious whole while using actors of widely differing origins. One must never lose sight of what one wants in the long run. A foreign actor is chosen because he has the face of the character one wishes. If the character is Italian, the actor will become Italian. There is not a great deal to be done about it— either he does become Italian or he doesn't. The problem is to get rid of everything about him that suggests his native country, to give him Italian gestures, Italian behavior, an Italian walk. This is an instinctive thing, it has to be polished up little by little.

I could give you many instances of occasions when I had to resolve serious problems in my relationships with actors. I should like at least to mention one of them in order to return to the question of intelligence in actors: the case of my relationship with Betsy Blair [who plays Elvia in *Il Grido*]. She is a very intelligent actress, who demands very elaborate explanations. I must confess that it was with her that I spent one of the most agonizing times in my career as a director; it occurred when she wanted to read the scenario of *Il Grido* with me. She wanted me to unveil the meaning behind every speech—which was, of course, impossible. Speeches are the fruit of the instinct; they are suggested by imagination, not by reason, and they often have no other reason for existing than the need felt by the author for just those words and no others. This is a perfectly natural fact, inherent in the nature of literary creation, and for that very reason often inexplicable.

Thus I had to invent purely imaginary explanations for Betsy
Blair, which corresponded in absolutely no way with what I meant
to say in the film, and at the same time try to understand what *she*
wanted to know. Only thus could I try to bring her to the point
where she could play the character better than if I had explained
it to her.

With Steve Cochran [who plays Aldo] I had to use the opposite procedure. He had come to Italy thinking—who can say
why?—that he might try to become a director, which was quite
absurd. And so he refused from time to time to do something, the
necessary motivation for which, so he said, he could not feel. Thus
I was forced to direct him with gimmicks, never letting him understand what I expected of him, but working with methods the existence of which he never suspected.

III

ANTONIONI'S WORKS

●

"Uno dei Nostri Figli"

This treatment, written by M. Antonioni, G. Bassani and S. Cecchi d'Amico, was to be the basis for the Italian episode in *I Vinti*. The Government refused to give the producer the subsidy that he had requested if the funds were to be used on this story, and it was never filmed. Antonioni had to shoot another story, which was prepared in haste and with which he has said that he was dissatisfied. The treatment was published, in Italian, in *Cinema*, July 25, 1954.

1.   Rome. The Galleria Colonna. A young couple enters a business office. The boy, Arturo Botta, is pale and sickly-looking; he is barely out of his adolescence. The woman, Mirella Lombardi, is twenty-two, and her placid, blooming looks contrast with the liveliness of her black eyes and her clear, sharp voice.

It is the woman who asks the attendant whether the director is in and whether they will have to wait long to see him. They are shown into a dark, echoing waiting room, where they are left alone.

The boy, who has a package in his hands, approaches the window and looks out without letting himself be seen from outside.

Under the arcade, the usual activity has quieted down a bit by this time of day. The attendant returns and asks them to wait a moment. The woman engages him in a conversation about the working hours of the office and other such subjects. The boy has lit a cigarette and he continues to look out the window. Suddenly his gaze becomes more attentive and concentrates on one point. At the window opposite, two boys are chatting in a relaxed way. One makes a furtive gesture in Botta's direction. Arturo turns back to-

ward Mirella, who is still chatting with the attendant at the wait-
ing-room door. The girl winks to Arturo imperceptibly, then re-
sumes her conversation with even more warmth than before; the
attendant becomes more lively too. Suddenly we hear a muffled
noise, followed by an explosion and cries coming from outside.
Terrified, the attendant looks toward the window.

"What's going on?" he cries, on the run.

Arturo Botta steps away from the window, out of which, as we
can see from his movements, he has been leaning. The attendant
takes his place, and we can now see that the two boys at the opposite window have also disappeared. A hail of multicolored handbills is falling under the arcade.

"Let's go down and see. Let's go down and see. What's happened?" cries Mirella, pretending astonishment.

Arturo Botta says nothing. He can neither speak nor pretend.
He is pale and trembling from head to toe. Mirella, who has taken
him by the arm, drags him out while the attendant at the window
tries to catch hold of one of the handbills.

Downstairs in the Galleria we find movement, smoke, and two
policemen rushing by in their dress overcoats and parade swords.

The bomb and the tracts have not made a great impression.
Most people have not even noticed that there was a bomb. They
heard some noise; that was all. Picking up the tracts, or glancing
at them without even taking the trouble to pick them up (*"Italians!—"* we read—*"Today, the 28th of October of the year XXIX of
the Fascist Era, the legion . . ."*), the idlers who frequent the
Galleria grumble, "Oh why don't they go . . ."

2. Mirella Lombardi walks along rapidly, holding Arturo's arm.
Arturo's face is grimacing and pearled with sweat, despite the bit-
ter coldness of the day. They have reached the Triton Square.
Mirella abruptly detaches herself from him.

"*Ciao,* see you tomorrow," she says, still playing her part with
conviction.

The boy looks at her, his face expressionless.

"And don't be late, now," the young woman adds, before moving away at an even stride.

Arturo nods agreement and sets out again. Suddenly he starts

with fright. Someone has taken him by the arm and is speaking to
him. She is a saucy little girl of seventeen, cute and open-faced.
She has surely seen the other girl, if we are to judge by her expression.

"So that's why I wasn't supposed to come?" she asks Arturo
timidly. He is still trembling with nervousness and shock.

"Mimma, what are you doing here?"

The young girl seems to be profoundly saddened by this remark. But the boy does not give her time to say anything. More
policemen have arrived and are now dispersing the few spectators
attracted by the incident. This is enough to revive Arturo's energy,
and he asks the girl to come away quickly, as quickly as possible.
They set off again, walking rapidly, although in fact they have attracted no attention, still talking animatedly, the boy ahead, the
girl following in a seemingly half-hearted fashion.

Mimma had received a mysterious coded message from Arturo.
In it, he told her that they could not spend the afternoon together
and begged her not to go to the Galleria for any reason whatever
after seven o'clock, but to stay home and wait for a phone call and
get hold of the key to the barge that her father owns on the Tiber.
The young girl, both worried and fascinated, has obviously rushed
straight to the Galleria and surprised Arturo as we have seen.

"I've got other things on my mind besides women," Arturo explains as they continue to walk along at a fast clip. "I wrote you
because I didn't want you to run any risk. You didn't see what
happened, then?"

"What?"

"The bomb. Run, move along, for the love of God!"

"What?"

"I've got to hide . . . Quick! Did you bring the key to the
barge?"

"Yes."

They take a taxi. Mimma is very eager to ask more questions.
But Arturo points to the taxi driver with a meaningful gesture.

"Lungotevere Flaminio, please."

The taxi takes them rapidly down the Via Tomacelli, in the direction of the river and the quays. Arturo sinks down in the seat.
He is perspiring and growing paler and paler.

"Is something wrong?" Mimma asks.

Angry, Arturo sits up and energetically shakes his head.

3. They get out of the taxi near the former Naval Academy.
Arturo notices Mimma's questioning look and explains that you
never should have yourself driven where you are really going. He
sets out again on foot, first casting circumspect glances in all directions. The girl pays the taxi fare and then catches up with him.
They soon arrive at Mimma's father's swimming barge. After making sure that no one has followed them, Arturo begins to climb
down the small stairway, behind Mimma.

The place is closed. But the girl has the key and they enter. It
is cold. Does Arturo really intend to spend the night here? Mimma
looks at her fiancé with almost maternal tenderness. But why does
he do this sort of thing? She feels as if she were living in wartime,
without there being a war. Her father also takes an interest in
politics, but only at election times, she says. Arturo replies that he
has no desire to take Mimma's father as an example. He says this
in a tone of voice that angers the girl, and he adds—he keeps
getting up every minute to peer outside—that war is the natural
condition of the male; as far as he is concerned, he has vowed himself body and soul to the struggle. Any other element in his life,
even love, can only be a facet of that incandescent prism; she must
understand him.

Mimma does not understand him, but she loves him too much
and she is so deeply touched to see him in this trembling, over-
excited state, that she says yes, she is willing to be a facet of the
prism. She wants so much to kiss him. . . .

4. *"Italians! Today, the 28th of October of the year XXIX of the
Fascist Era, the legion . . ."*

A police official is closely examining the tracts and comparing
them with others of a slightly different format. The examination
does not satisfy him, judging by his expression. The lettering is
different and the other tracts have a swastika at the top. A second
official, standing beside the first, asks him whether they are dealing with Nazi sympathizers.

"Not even that," the other answers, "They're Aryans . . . the
chosen race . . . the sun-men. That doesn't mean anything to

you? If you feel like it, put on your dark glasses and go take a look at them. For the time being, let's worry about this bunch."

He gets up and goes into the next room: "Tell De Vico to come here, and come yourself; have a look."

In the other room, a group of young men are waiting; among them, we recognize the two boys who were standing at the Galleria window when Arturo threw the bomb.

"Hello, boys," the commissioner greets them gaily. "Now let's sit down and have a little chat. Okay?"

5. The young dynamiters meet secretly in a furnished room rented by Lucio, a student at the university.

We find Ernesto, Mirella and her husband there the following day. They are thumbing avidly through the morning papers that Ernesto has just brought in. Ernesto has the raucous, piercing voice of a news vendor. He is the illiterate, the foot soldier of the company, the faithful executor of other people's orders. As for Mirella's husband, Antonio, he has the serious, priestlike look of a potential hero. This is also the way Arturo describes him to Mimma, explaining that he once served in the X Mas (the elite corps of the Fascist navy); he is now hunted by the police. Mirella's parents—she is the daughter of General Simonetti, a fervent monarchist—do what they can to help him.

At present, Antonio says, he is opposed to the Party's policy; they are getting soft and are in the process of drifting toward democracy. But—as Arturo tells Mimma—he will be able to awaken them; he is an ace and he has chosen collaborators like himself (Arturo), who are ready for anything.

Arturo enters, giving the Fascist salute; the others return his salute with a great deal of seriousness, but without interrupting their reading.

"What do the papers say?" he asks immediately.

"There's nothing, nothing; the bastards . . ."

Antonio throws the papers down on the table, which is piled with half-completed "packages" and with a kind of blackish granular powder: explosives.

Antonio has gone back to work on the "packages" when Arturo suddenly cries out. He has spotted the news item—a few lines among the murders and kidnapings. The bombing episode has earned an ironic paragraph in all the papers. Every shade of opinion has joined in a conspiracy to minimize the affair.

Ernesto breaks the silence and asks Antonio, "What did they think about it at the Party?"

Antonio makes a vague gesture. "Don't worry yourself. I'm the one who's in touch with the leaders. Your job is to carry out my orders. That's all," he answers, his air enigmatic and authoritarian.

"But did you talk to . . . ?"

Antonio cuts him off drily. "What do you want, official backing, published in the paper? For doing . . . Don't be so naive."

He goes on to say that one failure cannot be permitted to take the wind out of their sails. They will have to hold on. Arturo breaks in to explain that the thing to do is take advantage of this failure to intensify their activity, to widen its range, not to give the least hint of softness.

Mirella, who is more moderate, has a more political view, thinks that it is not yet time to install "the new order"; the "man" to lead it has not yet appeared.

But Arturo insists. He does not believe in historic conjunctions of circumstances; as for the "man," it is his belief that leaders are forged in action. The other replies that this kind of action never has anything more than very limited value in achieving their goal.

"You are the shopkeepers of history," she cries, "and right now you can't even manage to stir up public opinion."

Arturo is becoming excited in his turn, and replies, "Nobody wants to stir up public opinion. I don't give a damn about it myself, about the opinion of all the outcasts of society. We are the aristocrats of the mind. We don't throw bombs to make martyrs among our enemies but to show them our scorn; the martyrs, eventually, we're the ones who . . ."

And instinctively he turns around to look at a small notice stuck up on the wall behind him. On it we read: "The first duty dictated by nature to the males of the race is not to live, but to triumph or die." Other posters and declarations decorate the room, which resembles a real revolutionaries' den.

Antonio brings the conversation back to the practical level. He thinks there can be no doubt that they will have to intensify their activity. "Besides, we're not the only ones who want it," he adds, showing them telegrams sent by comrades in Milan, Palermo and Naples. He reads one of them aloud, picked at random: "We are sure the good weather will bring new laurels. Continue. *A Noi.*"*

"The good weather," Ernesto mutters under his breath.

"Idiot," Arturo answers. "Maybe one day you'll remember the code. That means plastic bombs."

"Oh, yes, sure," says Ernesto, who then settles down to listen diligently to Arturo's explanation.

"Today, we're sending packages of plastic off to the other sections. It's indispensable to show them that the Organization is continually expanding and widening its range. Then we'll go over the details of a new action which will show the world that there still exist some real Italians who haven't forgotten what the word honor means. We'll go into action when the police have finished investigating. As long as they keep Lucio behind bars, we've got to watch out."

At that very moment, Lucio knocks at the door in the usual way and then rushes into the room. He looks very pleased with himself. He is the kind of boy who thinks of himself as clever.

"I've seen them," he says.

"They questioned you?"

"Of course—but I've got a watertight alibi. There was nothing they could do to me."

To make a long story short, it is Lucio's opinion that the police haven't got a lead to follow. They are not at all under suspicion.

Arturo becomes impatient. What are they waiting for, then? They ought to go into action right away. The rhythm of revolutionary activity has to be sustained. Before another week passes, something really serious has to happen in Rome. They need explosives, lots of explosives, and the supply of plastic is exhausted. A little trip to the country is in order. That evening a coded message will be sent to their comrade in Palestrina. They will go see him the day after tomorrow.

Lucio announces another interesting bit of news. The editor of the magazine *Mare Nostrum* was one of the suspects arrested, but the police have had to let him go. The magazine is in the process of

* The traditional Fascist salutation.

making up a new issue, and Lucio is to write an article for it. Lucio knows his subject very well. The title of the article will be: "We love our country to the point of despair."

Lucio becomes the center of attention. Arturo, who deep down is jealous of Lucio's adventure, decides to bring the attention back to himself. He will organize the trip to Palestrina. To give the outing an innocent look, he will take a girl along with him: Mimma, a new recruit, a thoroughly trustworthy comrade. In the modest furnished room papered with sublime slogans, skulls and daggers, everyone is enthusiastic, even euphoric. Everyone feels himself swept along by destiny toward a utopian tomorrow.

6. We hear about this same utopian tomorrow again from the mouth of an unknown young man speaking at a student meeting.

Students walking down the pathways of the university, on the lookout for an excuse to skip their classes, stop before the orator. He often mentions "Our Party," the only representative of the real Italy, "that of Amba Aradam and Bir el Gobi, the Italy we are going to rebuild, no matter what the price; we especially, the students, the symbols of the race . . ."

At the orator's side, Lucio applauds frantically. Many others applaud along with him. A few protest, whistle, cry, "Reactionaries!" Lucio, who has picked out one of the hecklers, insults him. Quickly they come to blows. Ten or twelve students join in, fighting violently. A little to one side, a man watches them in silence. He exchanges a look with the orator, who immediately climbs down from the fountain on which he had been standing and moves away. The man continues to watch the brawl, satisfied with the result.

7.   Mimma's family lives in a modest apartment in the Via Cavour. Her father is the owner of the broken-down swimming barge, which is open only in the summer. In the winter his activities run the gamut from overseeing his wife's little dry-goods shop to minor repair work on electrical equipment. He is an old Socialist worker and a member of the Italian Socialist Party, in which he is active during the off-season.

Her family resembles thousands of others in every country: all share the same myths from one end of the world to the other—for instance, a preoccupation with their progeny's education. The children must go to the university. Mimma is in her first year there. Her father and mother, though the latter is less obvious about it, are very proud of this, which makes them favorably disposed toward their daughter's school friends.

This is why Mimma's father, Mr. Molteni, immediately grants the permission Arturo has just requested: to allow Mimma to participate in a students' outing that will last into the evening. He has noticed the slightly snobbish air about Arturo and the neo-Fascist insignia in his buttonhole, but he merely smiles and, pretending not to understand, asks, "What's that? A First Communion medal?"

8.   The police commissioner who had questioned the suspects at headquarters enters the betting parlor where Antonio works. Without hesitation he goes straight over to Antonio and offers him his hand. Antonio responds to his greeting very coldly.

"Lombardi, one of these days, I'm going to pull you in, and when I do, you'll stay a while, because I know perfectly well you get your kicks out of setting off little bombs."

Antonio gives him an ironic look. "Really, I don't understand what you mean, Mr. Commissioner. Besides, accusations have to be backed up with proof. I've always been taught . . ."

"That's just what we expect to get from you, and I bet it'll come soon. So long."

He walks away. On the doorstep, he bumps violently into a young man. He stops, face to face with Arturo. He looks him over. His look strays again toward Antonio, and, with a smile he says, "Hello, I'm delighted to make your acquaintance."

He leaves immediately. After a moment of confusion, Antonio and Arturo recover their wits. Antonio goes to the window to make sure the policeman is really gone. There is no one there. He leaves with Arturo, and together they walk to the car, where Mirella and Mimma are waiting for them.

9.   The four members of the expedition have rented an old jeep for the occasion. The objective of the expedition—which must keep up the appearance of a country jaunt—is the outskirts of Palestrina. Their comrades have already collected the new supply of plastic. They set out without incident. Mimma, in spite of herself,

is impressed by the style of the Lombardi couple (Mirella and
Antonio). She listens with admiration as they discuss their various
projects and the "Viminale Plan." She is delighted to see how
highly Arturo appears to be regarded, and at his skill in driving
the car; thus, when the moment of danger comes, she is entirely in
on the game.

For, in fact, Mirella notices that they are being followed: the
other car is a Topolino. They slow down, accelerate, turn into another road. There is nothing to be done about it. Implacably, always keeping the same distance, the Topolino continues to follow
on their heels.

Antonio has taken the situation in hand: he gives the orders.
Arturo feels himself slipping into a heroic atmosphere. The car
breaks away at a crazy speed along narrow roads where it is
barely possible to drive at all. Mirella, who is pregnant, complains
of being shaken up and asks them in vain to stop. Exasperated,
Toni slaps her, shouting: "A Fascist's wife doesn't have the right
to complain." Everyone is very much on edge. When they arrive at
Palestrina, they stop at a *trattoria* and wait to make certain they
have shaken their pursuers before they set out again. The Topolino does not reappear. Yet the tension remains high. Mirella is
angry, and Mimma is worried. At this rate they are likely not to
get back to Rome until very late, and she has promised to come
home before nightfall. But she does not have the courage to admit
this to the others.

The plastic operation is quickly taken care of, in an atmosphere
of perpetual conspiracy. Antonio is satisfied.

On the return journey, the fact that there are explosives in the
car forces them to drive more carefully. Everyone is more relaxed
and Antonio croons: "We will conquer, we will conquer, we will
conquer, on land, on sea, and in the air. . . ."

As soon as she comes home, Mimma receives a few slaps from
her mother, who is furious at her lateness. Her father comes to her
defense: "I'd like to know what you were doing at her age. . . .
Leave her alone . . . Long live free love. . . ."

Having left the Lombardis at their house and the explosives at
Lucio's, Arturo is driving the car to the garage when again he sees
the Topolino on his tail. A cold sweat breaks out on his forehead.

It is obvious that the unknown pursuers have not lost sight of him for a moment and that there is a possibility of their discovering the plot before the scheduled time of the bombing.

Controlling his nerves with difficulty, he manages to appear relaxed and, without getting out of the car, drives back to the betting parlor where Antonio works.

The Topolino stops behind him. Two men (one of whom we have already seen at police headquarters), get out, enter the parlor after Arturo and pretend to be betting on a horse.

Arturo speaks to a friend in a loud voice, then whispers under his breath, "Take the car back to the garage for me."

Arturo then goes out immediately. But, instead of returning to the car, he turns the corner and runs away at top speed. When the two policemen turn the corner after him, Arturo has disappeared.

One of the policemen shakes his head. "I really don't understand why they make us run after these brats. A little bomb from time to time never bothers anybody at all."

10.   It is not so simple a job to put together bombs that will go off in the Viminale in the middle of a full-scale political demonstration. Very complicated bombs with clockwork movements are needed. All the work is done in the furnished room, under Antonio's supervision. He became an expert on the subject during the struggle against the partisans, at the time of the "Social Republic."

One morning an incident occurs that throws all their plans into confusion. The neighbors have already complained about the noise the conspirators make during the night and about the junk of all kinds that they throw out the window. This particular morning, Mirella dropped a package containing leftover bits of plastic onto the balcony below; the neighbor's chickens scratched at the package, with the consequences that one would expect. It is some time later, and the voice of a man on the landing outside is threatening: "Open up! Open up! We're going to settle this!"

The young dynamiters hold their breath: the police! Barricaded in the room, they maintain their silence for hours and hours at a stretch. Night falls. Mimma becomes desperate. She absolutely has to go home. But Antonio is inflexible. Arturo, for whom they have been waiting all afternoon, arrives in the middle of the night.

After making him repeat the password several times outside the door, they open up for him.

He is unrecognizable. He is dressed all in black, a piece of mourner's crepe pinned to the lapel of his jacket (thus hiding the Fascist insignia that he cannot bear to give up wearing), his hair peroxided and crew-cut. He claims he is being watched and says that from now on he will be able to move about only at night. Since the Topolino business, he no longer feels at ease, and has decided it is a good time to assume a disguise. He is not afraid of jail, of course, but he does not want to be sent there before the job is done.

Besides, the problem of a meeting place must be solved. It is clear now, since the afternoon's incident, that there can be no possibility of their going on working in the same building. But where are they to go? Arturo has an idea. Mimma's father's swimming establishment. The young girl does not quite know what to say, she will do her best. . . .

The conspirators tiptoe out of the room, and each heads for home. The equipment is moved to Antonio's house, but only for tonight; any longer would be dangerous. The moving operation is begun as Mimma returns home, where more slaps await her for this unscheduled escapade.

11. The day, the time and the place of the demonstration are weighed and discussed at great length.

Work is now in progress in a room donated by the "D'Annunzians," a group which proves to be as valuable a set of collaborators as the former staff of *Mare Nostrum,* whose fervor extends to printing tracts to be distributed at the time of the bombing. Antonio has decided to force the party leaders to toughen up their policy and put all their efforts into bringing about the installation of the "regime" in the purest revolutionary style.

Five bombs are ready; Antonio has been working over them day and night; four are for the day of the bombing itself, while the fifth is to be used in a test. Arturo will make the test. Impatient, excited, hiding the bomb in a leather briefcase, he goes to pick up Mimma, whom he is to take along for the usual reason: to provide him the alibi of a lovers' outing.

They drive a Lambretta out to a deserted spot in the country. During the trip, Arturo does nothing but talk about the renaissance of myths, about Buddhism and about their leader, Julius von Evola, who is in prison just now. . . . Mimma is not particularly interested in all this. She would prefer another kind of talk, and she begins to feel that it is taking a long time to get to where they will make love. It is cold; she would like Arturo to slip a newspaper under his jacket to protect himself from the wind instead of pretending, in his summer suit, to be a little tough guy with muscles of steel and an iron will, a man "with a bronze torso, oaken hands and the soul of Garibaldi." At length, Arturo turns his scooter off onto a narrow, solitary lane and stops. Mimma, still impatient to begin kissing him, throws her arms about his neck.

"We've got to explode it," he says.

Mimma starts with surprise. "Explode it? Are you crazy?"

Arturo gives her a heroic, scornful smile and walks to the middle of the field without even listening to Mimma's anxious, maternal advice.

"Arturo, watch out!"

12. It is March 12. The great day has arrived. The sky is overcast, the dawn is gray. Our conspirators leap from a roof onto a balcony below; from there they slip along another balcony to the cornice of the building (it is in the Via Agostino Depretis opposite the Viminale) on which a bomb is to go off.

At the same moment, another conspirator, Ernesto, disguised as a wandering umbrella vendor, places a bomb in the crack between the wall and the sidewalk. He moves away as soon as he has finished his job. The street begins to fill with people. The explosion takes place an hour later. The largest bomb (over three and a half pounds of explosives), the one that was supposed to cause a massacre, does not explode. As for the other three, the first two, on the roof, cause negligible damage, and the third, the one set in the crack, does nothing but lift a car parked nearby and throw it against the wall. On the other hand, what does work marvelously well is the distribution of the tracts printed by the magazine *Mare Nostrum*. The Via Depretis is inundated by a veritable rain of paper as the conspirators flee the site of the bombing, each taking a different direction, as agreed in advance, to throw the police off the track.

13.   An hour later, at the political bureau in police headquarters, the commissioner and his colleagues are examining the tracts. To be more precise, they are comparing them with the first issue of *Mare Nostrum,* which came out several days before. Suddenly the commissioner exclaims with satisfaction, "That's it!" And, indeed, the letter *n* in the tracts is crooked, just as it is in the magazine. Here, finally, is the proof they have been waiting for. Nothing remains to be done but to follow this clue, and the guilty parties will easily be found.

"Let's go," says the commissioner, as he gets up.

Toward the end of the afternoon, in another part of the political bureau, about twenty young men—among whom we recognize all our conspirators except Antonio and Arturo—are lined up along the four walls. They have all turned their backs in order to avoid one another's gaze and the possibility of giving one another away by a gesture of recognition. Standing in the center of the room, the commissioner is beginning to question them.

"Now, boys, have we made up our minds? I've got forty more of you to question in the next room. Come on, Ernesto, tell me where you got the plastic!"

"Viva il Duce!" cries Ernesto.

The commissioner makes a gesture of weariness.

14.   Taking everything into account, Arturo Botta almost regrets that he has missed the opportunity to scrawl swastikas on the walls of the Regina Coeli Prison, along with his comrades.

The evening edition of the papers merely reports a large number of arrests, without conceding that the incident is of any special importance. And it's useless to count on the morning edition. Arturo is discouraged. He has gone to the university in hope of finding a little agitation there, but everything is calm, classes are proceeding normally. He has telephoned home to find out whether they have come to arrest him, but no one has asked for him. He had told his mother that he was going to spend the night out, and her only reply was to remind him not to forget dinner. He has spent the night in a flophouse; he felt safe there. He left at dawn.

He is now in the vicinity of the main railroad station. There is a public telephone in the arcade. He dials a number. After a long wait, the sleepy voice of one of the Party leaders echoes from the other end of the line. Arturo reveals his identity in the hope of being immediately congratulated for his courage. But the voice at the other end merely asks him what he wants. Arturo wants to know where Antonio is. His interlocutor thinks he is in hiding; he does not know, or pretends not to know, where. It is obvious that he wants to hang up, but Arturo insists. He wants to see the leader, to talk to him; he wants them to work out tactics together for making some political capital out of the bombing. The other's reaction is not very encouraging, but because of Arturo's insistence he condescends to meet him. Arturo is not to budge; he will join him in a few minutes. And so, shortly afterwards, we see them face to face. We have seen the Party leader before, at the university meeting, as he watched the student brawl. He is a cold, severe, shifty man. He seems completely insincere when he declares to Arturo that this is the very last time he is going to allow himself to be put in this kind of a spot. The Party needs men who keep a cool head, not half-mad enthusiasts. Arturo and his group may consider themselves expelled from the Party.

The color goes out of Arturo's face. He trembles, as he always does when he is moved. He protests his expulsion, summoning his most solemn vocabulary.

The leader looks him over and, changing his tone, says: "Try to understand. We're in a corner. We've got to let time work for us; everything works out in the end. The watchword is still the same: Keep the faith."

Arturo is too upset to catch the hidden meaning behind these words. One phrase rings in his ears: *excluded from the Party*—he, who thinks of himself as one of its purest heroes.

Abruptly he cries out that all Antonio's criticisms are correct; the Party is sinking into a middle-class doze, it is sliding down the slope toward democracy.

The leader gets angry in turn. "Enough of that now," he replies dryly.

He orders the young man to respect the hierarchy, to keep his trap shut. Besides, a passing pedestrian has approached and is watching them curiously. Arturo throws himself at the leader, to strike him, but the latter is much too strong for him. The whole thing is over in a few seconds. After throwing Arturo to the ground, the leader moves away and quickly disappears.

Mad with rage, Arturo wants to run after him, but suddenly depression gets the upper hand. A street sweeper has stopped close by; Arturo tries to get a grip on his emotions. In his present disordered state of mind it is difficult for him to summon the energy. Suddenly, his features harden; he has just made a great decision.

He runs to the telephone, dials Mimma's number. Talking to her, he becomes himself again, and he achieves the power to make the final gesture, the most sublime gesture of all. With this power in him, he expresses such thoughts as: "It is in the bloom of youth that nature intends the male to die. . . ."

From the tone of his voice, Mimma realizes that Arturo is getting ready to do something idiotic. Not even listening to her mother's scolding, she quickly dresses and sets out in search of him. She looks everywhere: at the homes of their mutual friends, at Party headquarters, at his parents' home. His parents are also beginning to worry; they have had no news of him since his phone call in the afternoon to tell them he would not be home to sleep. Mimma is desperate.

At the same time, at the edge of the Tiber, Arturo has just untied a boat from the swimming barge. He climbs in. He has been at pains to leave a large number of footprints on the sandy riverbank. Carried by the current, the boat drifts to the middle of the river.

Arturo takes a red, white, and green bandanna out of his pocket; it is a little flag like the ones used to decorate buses on national holidays. He ties it around his face like a gag. Then he gazes all around him for a long moment; there is no one on the shore. Arturo stretches out on the bottom of the boat, takes a revolver from his pocket and points it at his neck, sliding it as far around behind him as possible, so that he will seem to have been shot from the back.

The point of all this is to simulate a murder, the publicity from which will attract attention to all the other martyrs for the cause, to those who are forgotten as they languish in prison cells, and will finally rekindle the fervent flame of combat in the hearts of the slumbering faithful. He wants to give all those whom life has disappointed a martyr to revenge, an enemy to fight; if the enemy is too cowardly to act on his own behalf, why, then, one must act in his place! And the final point is this: to display himself, his unappreciated heroism, the life that he has always been able to live so dangerously, in their proper light.

Arturo has finally got himself into the right position. When, as he makes the final gesture, he raises the revolver to his neck, his hand does not tremble.

The boat glides silently along, carried by the current. A sharp crack. The boat continues to glide. On the riverbank, nothing has changed, there is no sign of life. No one has heard.

15.   Some hours later, the shore is alive with policemen, reporters and photographers, all elbowing for space around the boat. Everyone is wondering whether the inquest comes under the authority of the political bureau at Central Headquarters, or the district squad, or the local police.

Farther up, alone on the road, Mimma watches, her eyes filled with tears.

From Le Amiche

The street in front of the trattoria. Exterior. Night.

347.   Rosetta comes out of the *trattoria* and looks down the street.

348.   Lorenzo is walking away, his hands in his pockets. Rosetta starts to run to catch up to him.
        ROSETTA: Lorenzo!
    Lorenzo goes on walking without answering her call.
        ROSETTA: Lorenzo!

349.   She has almost caught up with him; at last she is next to him. They walk on at a jerky pace.
        ROSETTA: Lorenzo, I beg you, stop. I can't walk fast. I have high heels on.
    Lorenzo goes on walking, indifferent.

ROSETTA: Look at me, darling.

350.   Lorenzo stops short. Rosetta is frightened by this abrupt stop. She stumbles, then regains her balance by taking hold of Lorenzo's arm. Lorenzo does not take his hands out of his pockets.

LORENZO: What do you want? Go back to them.

ROSETTA: No, I don't want to see them any more.

LORENZO: Go home then.

ROSETTA: No, I'm going with you.

LORENZO (irritated): Where?

ROSETTA: I don't know. Calm down. I'm not going back home; that's all over.

351.   Lorenzo begins to walk again. Rosetta hangs onto his arm and leans her face against his sleeve. She rubs up against him lovingly.

ROSETTA: We'll stay together always. You mustn't ever suffer again that way; oh, I understand now—you needed me.

Again, Lorenzo stops short.

LORENZO: Rosetta, I have to tell you the truth.

352.   Rosetta is terrified.

ROSETTA (in a whisper): What?

LORENZO: I don't need anybody.

Rosetta stands there watching him, her eyes wide, pale, petrified, as if she were seeing him for the first time.

353.   Lorenzo goes on looking at her for a moment longer. Perhaps he would like to add something. Then he makes up his mind and abruptly walks away.

354.   Sound of receding footsteps. Rosetta stands there listening to Lorenzo's footsteps as they fade and then die away into the silence of the night, but she no longer tries to follow him; neither does she turn back.

355.   A moment later, Rosetta sets out again; she is desperate. She walks almost without paying attention to where she is going, absorbed by a single thought: the failure of her love. She weeps. A

nine-year-old girl, shivering in an old overcoat, stops and stares at her with great curiosity.

356.   Rosetta walks off sobbing. The child goes on her way and then turns around again to look at Rosetta.

DISSOLVE

Banks of the Po. Exterior. Morning.

357.   People have gathered on the embankment and are watching what is going on at the riverbank. Cars are parked there; among them are an ambulance and two police jeeps. Two medical orderlies are climbing up along the riverbank, carrying a stretcher on which lies a body covered with a sheet.

DISSOLVE

The fashion house. Interior. Morning.

360.*   The head of the house is present, with several customers. She is making sure that everything runs smoothly following the opening the day before.

   The models are walking up and down again, but less vivaciously than at the opening.

361.   Clelia and Momina appear in the doorway. They are both tired, and neither speaks. The directress calls to Clelia.

> THE DIRECTRESS: Clelia! The countess would like to see Number Forty-eight and the suit with the ermine. Isn't that right, Countess?

362.   There are about fifteen women grouped about the couches, chatting. Clelia looks at them.

> THE DIRECTRESS: Did you hear, Clelia?
> COUNTESS LANZI: There were two with ermine, one . . .
> CLELIA (expressionless): Yes, but I recall quite well, it was the one with a jacket that you liked.
> COUNTESS LANZI (flattered): What a memory!
> THE DIRECTRESS: Oh, yes, Clelia is extraordinary. Since

---

* 358 and 359 were eliminated in the final version.

she's been with us, we've all been able to treat ourselves to the luxury of forgetting things.

A SEAMSTRESS: Mrs. Janier called. She says she confirms her order for the "Spring" model, but she asks if we can put off the fittings for two weeks, because she's trying to lose some weight.

CLELIA (still expressionless): That's fine.

Clelia goes back to her customer.

363.   At the same time, Clelia is following the conversation between a middle-aged lady customer and a model. Fascinated, the customer is observing the thin, graceful young woman and feeling the material of the dress displayed on her wasplike figure.

THE MIDDLE-AGED CUSTOMER: And what is your waist measurement?

THE MODEL (proudly): Twenty-three.

Clelia sees that the customer is disappointed, almost angry, with this answer. She speaks to the model immediately, feigning astonishment.

CLELIA: What are you saying, Jeannine? You mustn't exaggerate. Twenty-six, you meant.

THE MIDDLE-AGED LADY (with satisfaction): Yes, it did seem to me . . .

THE MODEL (aside to Clelia): But I tell you . . .

CLELIA (dryly): You think you know the dresses better than I do? (then to the lady) It could be let out a bit. You'd need only a very little extra . . .

THE MIDDLE-AGED LADY: I would want to have it as an exclusive.

CLELIA: Naturally. I'll make a note of that.

364.   Clelia moves away from the mortified model. The model says once more in a childish voice:

MODEL: All the same, Miss . . .

CLELIA (to the model): Oh, I know perfectly well, a twenty-three waist.

Clelia turns toward the interior of the workshop.

CLELIA (in a new tone of voice): Push the little dresses, the simple ones.

THE DIRECTRESS: That's enough, I imagine. I would have liked to show some elegant cocktail dresses.

CLELIA: They don't do as well. In Rome, the women want to spend very little and seem very rich; here they may spend a great deal, but they want to look casual, offhand . . .

THE DIRECTRESS: Why?

The directress breaks off to greet Momina deferentially as she enters.

THE DIRECTRESS: Madam . . .

Momina replies with a discreet nod and then speaks to Clelia, under her breath and with a tone of slight complicity.

MOMINA: Did you know?

Clelia acknowledges this with a sad look, her eyes full of tears. The directress has noticed nothing and asks Momina to sit down.

THE DIRECTRESS: Take a seat, please; you wanted to see something for afternoon wear, didn't you?

MOMINA (to the directress): Yes, that's right.

The directress walks away and speaks to a model.

MOMINA (to Clelia): They've taken her to the morgue. They say she's all swollen up—almost unrecognizable. Imagine, what a horrible thought!

CLELIA (in a violent whisper): Shut up!

Momina looks at Clelia in surprise.

MOMINA: We shouldn't have left her alone. She'd be alive right now.

CLELIA (in a louder voice): Shut up! Get out! Just do one thing for me, get out!

The directress turns around and looks at Clelia. The other women also turn around, in surprise.

MOMINA: Don't get hysterical on me. What can you be thinking? It's harder on me than on you that she's dead.

CLELIA (no longer trying to control herself): Yes? Yes? And yet you did everything in your power to push her into killing herself. Everything! I remember when you advised her to go with Lorenzo. You even gave her the keys to your apartment so that . . . so that . . .

Momina has taken Clelia by the wrist, but the latter breaks free
with a sudden jerk and begins to push Momina toward the door.
The directress rushes up to the two women.

> CLELIA: To me, you're a murderess, a murderess, do
> you understand? You killed her with your advice, with
> your cynicism. . . .

The directress takes Clelia by the shoulders and tries to hold
her back. The other women have rushed up to help Momina.

> THE DIRECTRESS: Clelia! Has she gone mad? What's
> going on?

A model enters wearing an organza dress; she is very young; she
stops, stupefied, in her tracks, to watch what is going on.

> CLELIA (hysterical): If she hadn't been there, Rosetta
> would still be alive. She's a monster! She's worse than
> a killer . . . I have to say it! I don't care, I must say it!

With considerable effort, the directress has managed to take
Clelia by the shoulders and push her a little distance away. Clelia
is sobbing, not reacting to anything, abandoning herself totally to
her emotion.

> THE DIRECTRESS: What's going on?
> CLELIA (desperate): Rosetta.

Clelia hides her face in her hands.

> MOMINA (also overwhelmed with emotion): Rosetta
> Savone has committed suicide.

368.* During the past minutes, the women have approached and
now surround Clelia and Momina.

> A WOMAN (moved): Such a pretty girl . . .
> ANOTHER WOMAN: And so rich . . .
> ANOTHER WOMAN (severely): It's unthinkable . . .

369. Clelia uncovers her face. She is pale. Her features are tense
and contracted. She is no longer an elegant woman who knows
how to keep herself under control, but a woman of the people,
with spontaneous reactions.

> CLELIA: No! All these things are thinkable! What things
> go on in this world that has no thought except for its

---

* 365 to 367 were eliminated in the final version.

distractions, that only thinks about its clothes, its filthy, beastly underbelly . . .

370.   She throws aside a scarf which she has been holding in one hand and it lands on one of the customers.

> CLELIA: This empty world! Where no one does anything, yet no one has time to think of others.

Momina is weeping.

> A WOMAN: But has she gone mad?
>
> CLELIA: The time it takes to come here, that time you can find!
>
> THE DIRECTRESS (firmly): That will be enough, Clelia.
>
> CLELIA: Yes, that's enough.

371.   She turns to leave. She sees a chair loaded with scarves and other accessories. She takes a pile of them and throws them on the floor.

> CLELIA: Enough! (then, with relief) Ah!

She goes off quickly and heads for the staircase. Among the pieces of fabric and the artificial flowers and scarves scattered over the floor, the women look at one another in outrage.

DISSOLVE

From *Il Grido*

Canal and marsh with dike. Exterior. Afternoon.

440b.   Andreina looks about her, then heads toward a group of bamboo-and-straw cabins standing a little farther along.

441.   A group of men stand unmoving on the strip of land that stretches before the huts. Andreina approaches and asks them something. We see the men consult together; then one of them lifts an arm and points to a cabin standing apart from the others, toward which Andreina heads.

442.   Aldo is sitting on a low stool outside the hut; he is repairing a rubber boot. He has already rubbed with sandpaper the spot that needs work, and now he is cutting out a piece of rubber to

cover the hole. Inside the cabin, we see a fisherman who is cooking a fish on a rudimentary stove. A call from offscreen distracts
Aldo from his work.

> ANDREINA: Yoo-hoo!

443.   Andreina approaches with a smile. She seems happy to see
Aldo; she leans over him and kisses him on the cheek. Aldo lets
himself be kissed, without responding.

> ANDREINA: What a welcome, hey! I was hoping for
> better than that.

Aldo squeezes a tube of glue and applies some to the spot he is
repairing, then he spreads the glue with his finger. While doing
this, he asks:

> ALDO: How is it you've come all the way here?
> ANDREINA: Because I wanted to.
> ALDO: Who told you I was here?
> ANDREINA: It's not the state of Texas, after all.

444.   There is a moment of silence while Aldo blows on the repair
job to dry the glue, but he breaks off to give Andreina a questioning look.

> ALDO: You have any trouble with the police?
> ANDREINA: What police? Oh!—(remembering) There
> were two who came by . . . but nobody's looking for
> you, take it easy.

Aldo finishes and gets up. Andreina mistakes the meaning of
this movement and says with a certain amount of satisfaction:

> ANDREINA: You know, we can go back by boat?
> ALDO: Where?
> ANDREINA: To my place. You wouldn't want to stay
> here anyway.
> ALDO: I'm fine here.
> ANDREINA: Here?

445.   She looks at the cabin. The fisherman inside gives her a
friendly look.

> ANDREINA: Well!

She looks about her, at the cabins sunk in the mud, the rags hung up to dry, the filthy children playing at her feet, and ends by saying:

> ANDREINA: I don't understand why things are so ter-
> rible around here.

446.   Aldo looks at her and examines her with a little more attention and sympathy, then says:

> ALDO: You're cured, it looks like.
> ANDREINA: I'm all right, thanks.

The cooking has filled the cabin with a dense cloud of smoke
that now pours out the door. Andreina speaks to the fisherman,
who is still busy at the stove.

> ANDREINA: Say, what kind of fish is that?
> THE FISHERMAN: It's dory. You want to try some?
> ANDREINA: I don't like it, but I'm so hungry. . . . Come
> on, Aldo, let's eat?

She goes into the cabin.

The fisherman's cabin. Interior. Afternoon.

447.   Inside, there are two beds. A piece of cloth hung across the
room halfway up the walls is used to gather the rainwater that
seeps through the roof. There is a table; and fishing rods and
other bits of tackle lean against the walls. Aldo, who has entered
behind Andreina, says:

> ALDO: You'll have to leave after you've eaten.
> ANDREINA: Me? I'm staying with you.
> ALDO: And where are you going to sleep?
> ANDREINA: You know very well I can find a bed.
> ALDO: (almost compassionately): You're still doing
> that?
> ANDREINA: No. In summertime, there's work even for
> women—threshing wheat, the hemp . . .

448.   The fisherman has set his fish out on the table on a piece of
wrapping paper. Andreina begins to eat. Aldo watches her, rather
at a loss for words. Then he observes:

> ALDO: But the money you make, where do you put it?
> ANDREINA: In the safest place of all: in circulation.

She chews away at her fish with appetite, then speaks to the fisherman.

ANDREINA: In your opinion, what kind of weather are we going to have tomorrow?

449.   The fisherman looks at the sky through the door and answers:

THE FISHERMAN: Sunny. Guaranteed.

DISSOLVE

Beach at the mouth of the Po. Exterior. Early afternoon.

450.   Aldo and Andreina are sitting on the sand on the bit of beach that lies between the sea, the Po and the fishing village. The scenery, transfigured by the faint light, is softly melancholy.

Andreina watches the sea waves mingle with the river water and stir the reeds along the banks. She points this out to Aldo, with all the wonderment of a child.

ANDREINA: Look how beautiful it is.

Aldo looks and agrees with a nod. Andreina observes him for a moment and says:

ANDREINA: Listen, I've known all kinds of guys, but one who enjoys life less than you . . .

451.   Aldo smiles. His tone is almost affectionate when he speaks.

ALDO: I wasn't always like this, you know; (then suddenly rousing himself) I remember once, we were setting up a mill near Ferrara . . . You ever been to Ferrara?

ANDREINA: I was supposed to go there once.

ALDO: Well, anyway, one Sunday, my friends came to pick me up . . .

ANDREINA: All men?

ALDO: There were girls too; what a question! So, in the end, the thing is, the others decided to go dancing. The girl with me was called Irma, and she said, "Why do you want to go to the dance hall? We're always dancing. Let's go in here instead." And so we went into the museum.

452.   Aldo stops. Andreina turns around to look at him. Seeing
that the man is not going to continue, she says:

> ANDREINA: And then?
>
> ALDO: Nothing. We saw the museum.

Andreina shifts her position abruptly, almost with irritation.

> ANDREINA: What kind of a story is that? It doesn't have
> an ending!

453.   Also does not answer. He takes a handful of sand and lets
it pour slowly through his fingers. Andreina makes another abrupt
movement.

> ANDREINA: Now, there, that's the kind of thing that
> drives me crazy. You start talking and then you stop.
> Always just as you please. If you do that at work . . .
> Work, my dear, doesn't wait on your convenience!
>
> ALDO: But, after all, that's never been a problem. Just
> the opposite. At the refinery I wasn't just another one
> of the beet pickers . . . I was one of the few with a
> steady job, I was in charge of the slag oven. I could
> see my house from there . . . and even my daughter
> playing in the yard.
>
> ANDREINA: You have a daughter?
>
> ALDO: Rosina.
>
> ANDREINA: When I have a little spare time, I'd like to
> try to have a daughter too.

454.   There is a pause; then she starts speaking again, in a melancholy tone.

> ANDREINA: I had it happen to me once, too. I got preg-
> nant, but it didn't come off. It would've been just too
> wonderful if it had worked out. Right now I'd be
> married and God knows where . . .

They both look at the sea in silence.

DISSOLVE

The cabin village at the mouth of the Po. Exterior. Morning.[*]

455.   It has just stopped raining. The sky is dark. Every now and

[*] This scene was cut before being shot. The two speeches in 456 were inserted
after 461.

then a gust of wind stirs up the grass and the reeds. The earth is
nothing but one vast sheet of water. The sea waves flow into the
canals where the fishing boats are lined up, and make them jump.
A group of fishermen stand motionless on the bank. Below lie the
cabins surrounded by mud.

456.   When one of the fishermen walks away, the others begin to
move too. Aldo is the last to leave, along with the fisherman with
whom he lives.

> THE FISHERMAN: I'm pulling out. I'm going to my
> brother's place in Contarina. He's going to raise seven
> kinds of hell, but what can I do? If it keeps raining . . .

He stops Aldo, who was about to speak.

> THE FISHERMAN: You can stay as long as you like. I
> really mean it, that way you can take care of the boat.

Grocery store of the village at the dike. Interior. Morning.

457.   Andreina stands in front of the counter looking at the grocer,
who is pointing to a card stuck on the wall behind her: IN THIS
SHOP, ANYONE WHO CAN'T PAY HAS GOT TO GO AWAY. The man adds:

> THE GROCER: And, besides, I don't know you.

At the same time, he is staring at her with obviously indecent
intentions. Andreina shrugs her shoulders.

> ANDREINA: You don't know me because you're seden-
> tary.
> THE GROCER (stupefied, almost angry): I'm what?

The village at the dike. Exterior. Morning.

458.   Andreina comes out of the grocery and walks in the direction of the cabins.

459.   As she passes by an open door through which the sound of
a record player can be heard, a woman comes out on the stoop
to look at her. Behind the woman we see, inside, an old phono-
graph on a chair. It is playing a French song of the twenties and
thirties.

> *On dit*
> *que je suis Mistinguett,*
> *C'est vrai!*

*On dit
que je suis une coquette,
C'est vrai!* . . .

Andreina walks on without listening. She is wearing her high-heeled shoes and walks as if each step were an exercise in balance. She has a touching and absurd note of elegance about her.

The cabin village at the mouth of the Po. Exterior. Morning.

460. Aldo and the fisherman have arrived at their cabin. They say nothing. The sky is growing darker and darker, the wind stronger, the rain nearer. Andreina appears from behind the slope that faces the cabin. Seeing them, the young woman cries out in a joyous, but forced, voice:

> ANDREINA: In this shop, anyone who can't pay has to go away (and she waves her empty hands).

461. The three meet and walk to the cabin together.

DISSOLVE

Cabin in the village at the mouth of the Po. Interior. Evening.

462. The cabin is full of smoke from the cookstove. Aldo is fanning the fire, but without conviction. Andreina is standing on one of the beds, trying to adjust the cloth attached under the roof so that it will protect them better against the rain, which is lightly falling outside. Some water has accumulated in the cloth, and Andreina pours it on the floor, then puts a bucket under the cloth. Then she remakes the bed on which she had been standing and says as she looks at it:

> ANDREINA: There's always something lacking; Now that I know where I can sleep, we haven't got anything to eat.

463. Aldo stops fanning the fire and opens the door because there is too much smoke. He takes a few steps outside, where it is now completely dark, then comes back in. The rain has slightly dampened his face and hair.

Andreina who has followed him with her eyes, says:

> ANDREINA: And if I weren't here, what would you do?

Aldo wipes his face with a handkerchief.

ALDO: I'd wait for the good weather.

ANDREINA: And when the good weather came?

Aldo looks at her as if he suddenly saw her in a different way.

ALDO: So you're the one who's giving me advice now. How old are you?

ANDREINA: Eighty.

ALDO: Well, I'm ninety.

ANDREINA: Fine. Well then, let's do one thing . . .

464.   Aldo does not let her finish. With a gesture that betrays both his irritation and the erosion of his will, he cries:

ALDO: No, we're not going to do anything.

After taking a few steps into the cabin, Aldo sits down on the bed. Andreina watches him as if she expected him to say more. But Aldo says nothing; he seems wrapped up in himself, as if she were not there. With bitter resignation, Andreina says:

ANDREINA: Okay, fine, I understand. If I don't take charge . . .

ALDO (half indifferent, half incredulous): Where do you think you're going? It's raining.

ANDREINA (ambiguously): For a walk.

465.   She runs a comb through her hair, then places the comb on the table as she puts on her coat. She walks to the door. There she stops.

ANDREINA: See you later.

She goes out and disappears into the darkness.

466.   Aldo throws himself onto the camp bed and lies there looking at the cloth under the roof. There is a hole in the cloth. Through this hole drops of water are falling into the bucket Andreina has put on the floor.

The village by the dike. Exterior. Evening.

467.   Andreina arrives at the slope that separates the cabin village from the village by the dike. The whole area is lit by only one lamp hung from a telephone pole. As she passes under the lamp, Andreina takes her lipstick out of her bag and begins to paint her lips, but mechanically, without even stopping. She continues walking and goes toward the spot where the grocery store is located.

Cabin in the village at the mouth of the Po. Interior. Evening.

468.   Aldo is growing more and more worried. He is still looking outdoors as if he were waiting for someone to return. Then he turns around; on the table he sees Andreina's comb. Aldo gazes at it with almost spasmodic tension. The wind is blowing the smoke back into the cabin, which is soon filled with it.

Aldo picks up the bucket under the cloth. He empties it onto the stove, and the fire goes out with a crackling, spitting sound. The smoke is even denser than before.

Then he goes out.

The cabin village at the mouth of the Po. Exterior. Evening.

469.   Aldo walks away from the cabin and runs toward the slope lit by the single lamp. The ground is slippery and full of pools of water that gleam in the shimmering light. Aldo runs without looking where he is going, and once he slips. He gets up covered with mud and, without cleaning himself off, begins to walk again, more slowly.

The town at the dike. Exterior. Interior. Evening.

470.   Aldo passes the slope and enters the village. He stops and looks about him; all the windows are shut and unlit. He calls out.
     ALDO: Andreina! Andreina!

471.   He goes on; he stops at another spot and calls out again.
     ALDO: Andreina! Andreina!

The door of the grocery store that we have seen before opens and Andreina comes out. The young woman has scarcely got out the door, when she finds herself face to face with Aldo, who is filthy, upset, out of breath.

Slightly irritated, Andreina asks him in a whisper:
     ANDREINA: What's the trouble? Why are you shouting?
     ALDO (still shouting): Go back to the house.
     ANDREINA: In the meantime, stop shouting. And then explain to me why I have to go back to the house . . . (there is a pause). You don't know why I came here. Because *I'm* hungry is why, and because *you're* hungry too. And if you deny it, you're a liar.

472.   Aldo looks at Andreina. Suddenly he stops speaking. He turns around and begins to walk away from her at a weary pace. The young woman follows him, a few steps behind, still shouting.

> ANDREINA: I'm a girl who's got no luck; but you—what do you take yourself for? You've had your share of tough breaks, I won't deny that. But it'd take me a month to tell you all of mine.

473.   Aldo quickens his step. Andreina follows him, but she is losing ground. They are now in a dark patch, where the light from the grocery penetrates only a little. We hear the voices of two shadows, Andreina's broken now by tears.

> ANDREINA: Where are you going now? Wait. Let's talk, can't we? Where are you going?

And she stops, seeing that Aldo is continuing on his way and not turning back. Suddenly she breaks into sobs that shake her whole body.

She looks once more in Aldo's direction.

474.   Aldo's silhouette disappears into the darkness.

475.   Andreina turns back in the direction from which she has come, still weeping. She heads toward the slope, passing in front of the grocery door. A man comes out of the grocery, the grocer who was talking with Andreina that morning. Leaning out to the young woman from the doorway, he calls to her in a whisper:

> THE GROCER: Hey!

Andreina turns around, her face covered with tears. She makes an abrupt movement.

> ANDREINA: And you can go to hell too, you!

She goes on walking, tripping now and then on the uneven, slippery ground.

From *La Notte*

The park of the villa. Dawn.

Giovanni and Lidia head silently for their car. They pass a fountain, at the edge of which Berenice is sitting with Giovanni's young admirer. Berenice is looking at the girl, who is watching a fleet of little paper boats floating in the water.

Resy is weeping softly. And as Berenice's look seems to ask the reason for her tears, Resy sighs.

> RESY: Oh, don't pay any attention. I'm only crying for something that isn't worth the trouble anyway.

Lidia and Giovanni set off again; Lidia stops for a moment, struck once again by the spectacle of the cat motionlessly staring at the statue of a child overturned on the field. Something about the animal's fixedness troubles her. But she goes on walking and soon catches up with Giovanni. They both cross the field, going toward the parking lot.

> LIDIA: Let's not go home right away.
> GIOVANNI: You're going to enjoy this—Valentina's father has asked me to work for him. He's offering me a top position.
> LIDIA: Well?
> GIOVANNI: I think I'm going to refuse.
> LIDIA: Why? It's a good opportunity.

Surprised, Giovanni looks at her. Lidia goes on:

> LIDIA: Taking everything into consideration, your life would be easier.

Giovanni puts his hand on the car-door handle; he opens the door and waits for Lidia to get in. Instead, she says, after a short pause:

> LIDIA: I called the clinic just now. Tommaso is dead.

Giovanni closes the door with a sharp crack. The news hits him hard. He walks a few steps away from the car. In the distance, across the countryside, the sky is beginning to grow pale.

> GIOVANNI: When? Why didn't you say anything to me?
> LIDIA: You were playing. (a pause) He was really a good friend, to you? To me he was much more than that. In his eyes, I had strength and intelligence that I'm sure I really don't have. But he was so convinced of it that I ended up believing it too.

She remains pensive for a few moments, as if lost in her memories. Then she begins speaking again, softly.

LIDIA: He spent so many days sitting beside me, at a table, making me study. And I had no desire at all to study, I was so absorbed in my own little problems; and then there he was, insisting, even pestering me. I got to the point where I hated him for it, for nothing else but that. And never once did he talk about himself. It was always me, me, me. And I never understood . . . never realized. Yes . . . you're so ridiculous when you're young, with that absurd inconsistency. You never imagine anything can end.

Lidia takes a handful of damp earth; she walks a few steps to a tree where the earth is drier. She sits down and Giovanni joins her; almost immediately, she begins to speak again. Quite near them there is a patch of water; there are many leaves lying on the surface.

LIDIA: You, on the other hand, you began by talking to me about yourself. That was something new, and I was so happy about it that nothing in the world could have seemed sweeter. (a brief pause) Perhaps because I loved you. Because I loved you, you and not him. And then in the end, his adoration irritated me, even if you were flattered by it . . . Isn't that true?

Giovanni admits that it is.

GIOVANNI: Yes, but not quite true either. He was so vulnerable. . . .

Some time passes. The dawn is rising slowly; a little light filters through here and there. A gleam on the water, on the damp leaves on the ground. Lidia rubs the bark of the tree, then looks at her reddened, dirty hands.

LIDIA: If I want to die, it's because I don't love you any more.

Another silence. Lidia takes a few steps, incapable of remaining motionless.

LIDIA: That's why I'm desperate. I'd like to be old

already, to have devoted all my life to you, I'd like not
to exist at all any more, because I can't love you. There,
that's the thought that came to me while we were at
the night club and you were being so bored. . . .

GIOVANNI: But if you say all this to me, if you really do
want to die, that means you still love me.

LIDIA: No, it's only pity.

Giovanni seems to be following some secret thought of his own.

GIOVANNI: I haven't known how to give you anything;
I haven't realized anything. I've wasted my life, and I
go on wasting it this way, like an idiot, taking, without
giving anything, or giving too little, in exchange. Perhaps I'm not worth much. If that's what you mean,
you're right.

LIDIA: I used to spend whole afternoons reading, sitting on my bed. Tommaso would come and find me
there. He could very well have kissed me. I wouldn't
have pushed him away—out of boredom. . . . But he
was satisfied to look at me, to listen to me as I read . . .
all those books that never did me any good for anything. Two hundred pages a day; I read very fast.

Giovanni looks at her with great tenderness. The dawn is becoming brighter. The jazz music goes on in a distant, muffled echo.

GIOVANNI: I haven't given you anything. It's odd that
I should realize only today that whatever we give to
others always ends by returning to us.

Lidia points to the musicians in the distance.

LIDIA: What can they be hoping for? That the day will
be a better one if they go on playing?

GIOVANNI: Lidia . . . Let's drop this discussion, let's
try to find support in something solid. I love you . . .
(as if he were discovering this feeling for the first
time). There. I'm sure I still love you. What more do
you want me to say? Let's go home.

Lidia sits down and opens her bag. She takes out a letter and starts to read.

> LIDIA (reading): This morning you were still sleeping when I woke up. I awoke very gently. I felt your light breathing, and through the hair that hid your face, I saw your eyes . . . and emotion gripped my throat. I wanted to cry out, to wake you, because your weariness was too deep, even deathlike. In the shadow, the skin of your arms, of your breasts, was so alive . . . I felt it, warm and dry, I wanted to press my lips to it, but the thought of troubling your sleep, of having you in my arms once again, stopped me; I preferred having you this way, like a thing that no one could take away from me . . . for I was the only one who knew it . . . an image of you for always. . . .

Lidia's face contracts with emotion as she reads. Giovanni keeps his eyes fixed on her, as if searching to rediscover both the emotions and the features described in the letter. Lidia goes on reading.

> LIDIA: Behind your face I saw something purer and deeper, in which I was reflected. It was you I saw, in a dimension that included all the time I have left to live. . . . All those years were there, but also all those I lived without knowing you, waiting to know you. That was the little miracle of this awakening—that I felt for the first time that you belonged to me, and not only for that one instant; that the night was not yet over, that it would stretch out forever beside you, in the warmth of your blood, of your thoughts, of your will, that mingled with my own. At that moment, I understood how much I loved you, and the feeling was so intense that my eyes filled with tears. Because I thought that it would never finish, that our whole life should be for me like this morning's awakening, feeling you not only beside me but forming a part of me, in a way nothing and no one could destroy, not even

La Notte: Jeanne Moreau as Lidia and Marcello Mastroianni as Giovanni.

the dulling influence of habit that I feel hanging over us like a threat. . . . And then you woke very softly and, still smiling in your sleep, you kissed me, and I felt I had nothing to fear, that we would always be the same as at that moment, united by something stronger than time, stronger than habit.

Lidia, overcome with emotion, looks at Giovanni defiantly.

GIOVANNI: Who is the letter from?

A silence. Then fixing Giovanni with her gaze:

LIDIA: You.

Giovanni is silent. He looks at her as if he were annihilated by the truth that Lidia has so pitilessly bared: for both, love is dead.

Lidia lets him stare at her. She is so shattered that she suddenly seems old. Giovanni draws her to him and tries desperately to kiss her. And Lidia lets him kiss her, while heavy tears pour from her eyes and wet her cheeks. Giovanni violently drinks her tears and throws her back onto the grass. He is on top of her. He embraces her, runs his hands over her face and neck, as if trying to recognize her.

LIDIA: No . . . no . . . no . . . I don't love you any more . . . I don't love you any more. And you don't love me any more, either.
GIOVANNI: Shut up! Shut up!
LIDIA: Say it! Say it!
GIOVANNI: No, I won't say it. I won't say it. . . .

Lidia closes her eyes and lets herself be carried away—it is something like an animal fury that seizes her—by the memory of what has been and what might yet still be again.

Their kisses speak their hope.

Under the awning, the musicians go on playing. It is a slow tune, in harmony with the sad birth of the new day.

IV

CRITICISM AND COMMENTARY

Publisher's Note: This section contains, in chronological order, critical writings from Italy, France and the United States. Reviews of individual films have for the most part been omitted in favor of more general criticism. Among the American selections, however, several excerpts from reviews of L'Eclisse (Eclipse) have been included because it was released after Pierre Leprohon prepared this book.

GIDEON BACHMANN

A Cinema of Behavior and of Interiority

JACQUES DONIOL-VALCROZE
[From *Cahiers du Cinéma*, October 1957]

I have just reread Pavese's novel, *Tra Donne Sole,* for the tenth time and am convinced that, in the present state of the cinema, it was not possible to make a faithful adaptation of it (as Antonioni tried in *Le Amiche*). The story has no visible dramatic progression, no external framework, no development in any of the characters, no thesis, not even a central idea or "message" that might have served as a starting point. Ten characters move confusedly through an almost indeterminate stretch of time, come, go, speak, take short automobile rides around Turin, separate, meet again, resume that lazy existence which brings together both idlers and employed. . . . The admirer of neatly tied-up scenarios has no choice but to flee all this.

Yet there is one principle of unity in the story: the narrator Clelia; and I am astonished that Antonioni did not take her as his point of departure, for it is through her eyes, even so, that the story is seen, through her temperament, her experiences and her judgments that it is presented. If there are obscure points in the story, they are justified by the fact that Clelia is recounting what she sees as she sees it, not yet knowing the full details regarding the group with which she has become involved. I have no doubt that this procedure was intentional with Pavese: the obscurity is planned, but the author has taken pains to justify it by means of the narrator's subjective view.

Giving up the "I" and adopting the "once upon a time" convention, Antonioni launches upon an impossible adventure. Now he has to explain everything, which is to say that, in the long run, he has to create a new story. In Pavese, a sort of hierarchy among the characters gradually emerges. Along with Clelia, Momina survives in our memory, the resigned Momina who is the only lucid member of the group, and Rosetta, Rosetta who is not so lucid but who is the only one not to give in to resignation, the only one who finally commits the act that breaks the rules of the game. The others remain what they are: fairly intelligent, very vegetable, disillusioned survivors of a little agonizing world. For this misty universe swept up in a cosmic movement that overtakes and smashes it, Antonioni has substituted a classical novelistic universe with angles, joints and traditional conflicts: Clelia's love for her profession and the ambition that overrules her love for the architect's assistant (Becuccio in the book); Rosetta's first and second suicides because of Lorenzo (Loris in the book)—a secondary character (like all the men in the story), now promoted to an important role with his own personal conflicts (his jealousy over his wife's artistic success).

And from this point forward, in a sense, everything collapses. Clelia is a strong character in the book; she knows where she is going and has an impressive inner serenity; Becuccio means no more to her than Febbo, the architect who makes love to her by chance one evening, in three minutes stolen during an escapade with Momina; she is beyond the possibility of degradation. Rosetta is a weak character, whose health and background prevent her from making the leap to the kind of independence and moral indifference that Clelia possesses; she kills herself, having succumbed to the great temptations of purity and the absolute. She is the premonitory double of Pavese himself, a convinced Communist but an anguished man, who, one year after writing of Rosetta's suicide in a Turin hotel room, killed himself, at the height of his career . . . in a Turin hotel room. The moving symbol of this existential contradiction is the sky-blue tulle dress that Clelia twice glimpses.

Antonioni forgot that Rosetta was basically that sky-blue creature. He added her impossible love for Lorenzo out of his own head, and without great success.

Yet while being faithless to the book, he sought with impressive stubbornness to save the Pavesian "climate" in the film. It is a not-so-surprising paradox that he did this best in the most thoroughly original parts: in the scene on the beach—a contraction of several sea scenes in the book—which Pavese would no doubt have found too systematically melancholy and choreographic, but which rings true. Or in the first love scene between Rosetta and Lorenzo on the street, so exquisitely relaxed and restrained. Antonioni is particularly successful in the depiction of the five women: Clelia, Momina, Rosetta, Nene and Mariella. In spite of everything, they are Pavesian. They come from no other source but his own imagination, they are cinematographically unique, and each has a great moment in which the screen is filled with an extraordinary fascination: Clelia, with a little smile, looking at Becuccio's image in a truck's rear-view mirror; Momina greeting Febbo in the stairway of her house; Rosetta confessing her love for Lorenzo with an overwhelming modesty; Nene saying to Rosetta, with heroic humility, "If I had had children, I wouldn't have given in"; Mariella, after being kissed by Febbo on the beach, joking about her suit covered with sand: "For us women, it's our skin that's our real clothes."

I have no regrets about having been a member of the Venetian jury which gave the prize to *Le Amiche*. At the time, I had never read Pavese and I had seen the film twice in a row without subtitles; in this way, I got the most Pavesian impression possible, without knowing the book and without being able to follow the dialogue closely. A week later, I plunged into *La Bell' Estate*. Seeing it again today, I do not find the same magic in the film. Pavese's genius has intervened and makes any attempt at illustration seem smaller. But *Le Amiche's* importance remains: it is an attempt to substitute for the cinema-as-spectacle a cinema of behavior and of interiority, to create a new cinematographic language, to set in motion an evolution toward a more mature form. Like many other seekers and innovators, Antonioni suffers all the hazards and difficulties of being first man in the territory he has chosen to explore—hazards which will of course be overcome in time; but even if there were only ten perfectly successful minutes in his film, he would still have earned our gratitude and respect. Dear Antonioni, his work so often challenged, so challengeable, but courageous and obstinate; perhaps he is doing no more than inserting a knife blade into the door that opens out onto hope and freedom. But since Bresson, we have realized that it sometimes requires no more than a spoon handle, and others will pour into the breach. Already, in *Le Amiche*, we have received a puff of air from another world. If only for that . . .

An Open Letter to Antonioni on *Le Amiche* and Pavese

ITALO CALVINO

[From *Notizario Einaudi*, Turin, November–December 1957]

I will admit to you that when I learned you were preparing to make a film out of *Tra Donne Sole* I felt a certain apprehension: it seemed to me that of all Pavese's novels, this was the least adaptable to the cinema, based as it is on a rigorous counterpoint composed of dialogue and feelings depicted in halftones, and on situations that seem too tense, too thorny, to be reproduced on the screen without distortion. Your film very largely destroys these apprehensions: a clever scenario uses and develops the elements of the novel in a finished cinematographic story which has its own logic and which even preserves a certain *Pavesian* flavor.

Le Amiche's principal merit certainly lies in being important as a film in itself, as *your* film, independent of *Tra Donne Sole*. The observation of manners and morals—which was of value to Pavese only insofar as it served as raw material with which to express his lyrical-moralist's vision of the world—now appears in the foreground, as indeed the cinema's proper mission requires. It is thus in harmony with the role of bitter chronicler of a middle-class generation that you have so felicitously played in your preceding films, and which here achieves its most complete expression. This is the first time that the cinema has shown the groups of men and women friends that are formed among the middle-middle classes of the cities; the atmosphere of evenings and Sundays spent together in social activities, in automobile excursions; the flashes of violence and bitterness that brew beneath the surface of light chatter. Here is a fully formed world which has already built up its own literary tradition, but which the cinema had never yet succeeded in dealing with, because the cinema seemed better suited to presenting stories that were rich in contrast; individual *exploits,* rather than the subtle lights and shades of life in society. You have captured this world with the dryness that characterizes your style, founded on the interplay between sad, wintry landscapes and a dialogue that is neutral, almost casual: a cinematographic style that recalls the lessons in understatement provided by so many modern writers, Pavese himself among them. Your contribution in this film lies in having been able to look at this world with a sharp eye, unaffected by indulgence (without the nostalgic, crepuscular ornamentation of Fellini's *I Vitelloni*), bringing pitilessly into the light the elemental cruelty, the superficial sensuality, the permanent cowardice in the face of the most demanding moral crises. And above all, not to have limited yourself to the portrayal of manners but to have contrasted with this world another rhythm of life, another rule: that of work, no matter what kind of work—whether running a high-fashion house or manipulating bricks and mortar—as long as it involves realizing oneself in something fully accomplished.

Experimental Directing

TINO RANIERI
[From *Michelangelo Antonioni,* 1958]

At first glance, it may seem that Antonioni's active contribution to the Italian cinema is limited to the second phase of neorealism, or rather, that it may be itself considered as the essential element in the rupture which, after 1950, separated the first examples of middle-class neorealism from the popular neorealism of the preceding five years. This is an inadequate view. The individualistic position, the splendid isolation in which some people like to see Antonioni, is less a point of departure than the outcome of a fully mature and fertile process of preparation in which neither human relationships nor the lessons of the masters have been neglected. If we hold Antonioni particularly dear, it is for this reason also: he seems to us to have been able so to condition his effective participation in the cinema that it does not emerge as a function of the simple demands of circumstances, but of a deliberately pursued personal transformation.

This is why he seems to us to have been detached from the adventurous climate that existed in the Italian cinema from 1945 to 1947. This is why, in contrast to Visconti, De Sica and Rossellini, from whom he is separated by an astonishingly slim difference in age, Antonioni is still a "young" director. He is still regarded as "full of promise" despite the established mastery of his style, which is one of the most obvious elements in his work. He has been defined, not without irony, as an "eternally experimental director." This definition is acceptable, but if it suggests a crucial problem for Antonioni as a man, it must not be taken as suggesting a limitation in him as an artist. For the present era is an era of men who are ceaselessly experimenting, ceaselessly preoccupied with the need to test and develop their own powers, continually conducting a trial in which they themselves are the accused. We live in an age of research, and the researcher in the field of emotion or of any other force, concrete or abstract, is a man who has accepted the fact that he lives a life of constant experimentation. In this sense, Antonioni is young and modern.

Those who have seen *Il Grido* will understand even better what I am alluding to. Perhaps, after *Il Grido*, Antonioni has said all he has to say; or perhaps his interior universe will succeed in expressing itself even more vigorously. But today he is, more than anyone else, the director of the world of *today* in Italy. And we are not, let us repeat, considering a point of departure. We are considering personal and fundamental points of "arrival," reached at the end of a long process of preparation.

Antonioni is the vanguard of a rehabilitation of esthetic theories within the framework of neorealism, a neorealism founded on enthusiasm, improvisation, feeling, reaction to feeling. We begin to understand why Antonioni was unable to associate himself with the neorealism of *Open City*, an inspired film but a rough one, with several different cadences, a film which might be compared to one of those elemental war songs, half-dialect, that make us shiver with patriotism but give short shrift to grammar. It was a cinema of solidarity and co-operation, but one in which improvisation played a pre-eminent role, in which sentiment, with all its hidden dangers, was ever present. When Antonioni's voice is first heard in the debate, it is the voice of a reasoner; the polemic element persists, but in a subtle form, stripped of every optimistic note. The difference lies in this: that we ourselves, all of us in the darkened theater, were able to provide the characters of the earlier neorealism with what they lacked, with what they demanded. But to the characters created by Antonioni we can give nothing; it is only within ourselves that we can bring them to completion, discover a source of light with which to illuminate them, by an extension of the intellectual process quite different from that to which the earlier neorealism had accustomed us. . . .

Today the cinema is sailing through troubled waters. But if there is anything at all that seems clear, it is the fact that Michelangelo Antonioni will be among the last to surrender; that the Italian cinema, though it lacks the rules that might lead it to salvation, also and fortunately lacks the rules that might lead it to its fall. It is abandoned to the temperaments of men, to the spirit of the times, to human disorder. It refuses inexorably to conform to any prediction. And if some have been able to see in *Il Grido* (and not altogether inaccurately) a kind of spiritual testament, we believe that it is less Antonioni's testament than that of an age or of a cinematographic school. Antonioni once again stands apart. He remains the observer of our times. We shall need others like him.

Only Here and Only Now

FABIO CARPI
[From *Michelangelo Antonioni*, 1958]

It is impossible not to notice the way in which Antonioni often resorts to a dramatic and final solution—murder or suicide. These are, in fact, two analogous ways of breaking all ties with society and life. Opposed to death as a solution, we find the compromise of work as a justification for one's personal existence (and solitude). And between the two? Between the two lie the illusion

"...some visual effects reminiscent of previous films,.."
From *L'Eclisse*.

Piero (Alain Delon) in *L'Eclisse*.

and the temporary comfort of love, which is one way of escaping solitude and communicating with others, even if the outcome is known and the failure foreseen in advance.

Now, are these pessimistic conclusions? Perhaps. At all events, we are dealing with an active, stimulating and touching pessimism, a point of view that ought not to be confused with Fellini's passive, twilight pessimism. The inability to communicate is pathological in Fellini; with Antonioni it is logical. Fellini believes in God; Antonioni believes—in spite of everything—in man. He believes in him so deeply that he is prepared to destroy him or sacrifice him—but never to condemn him. And how could he condemn him, after all, when his antireligious convictions lead him to deny every kind of transcendence and to seek for meaning in life *only here and only now*—in other words, in life itself?

Only here and only now. The words are worth repeating, because this almost physiological preoccupation with the need to adhere, sensuously, to the concreteness of the passing moment has made him turn away from the dramatic progression of facts and events (the method of the traditional novel) and to attempt to re-create for us the depth and the breadth of reality. In constructing his story, Antonioni has substituted a horizontal scheme (reality) for a vertical one (the action of the story); in the characters, he has replaced dependency (which lies in the domain of fiction) by autonomy (which is a characteristic of life). The autonomy of the characters, which is one of the most disturbing characteristics of the modern novel, implies their permanent "availability," but also their predestination, their calling, to solitude. Absolute autonomy cannot fail to coincide in a certain way with a rejection of human relationships. By several different routes, then, we return to the theme of solitude, a theme that Antonioni is ceaselessly developing, not in terms of a precise individual frustration, but in the sense of a collective curse weighing on man *now, today.* His pessimism stops at this point: at the point of *now, today;* it is neither religious nor metaphysical, but immanent, and precisely for that reason, beneficent.

Many people persist in accusing Antonioni of being cold because they are unable to bear his stubbornness in refusing to accept the validity of the traditional lower-middle-class idyl, with its

perpetual assumption of a happy ending—or, if absolutely necessary, a desperately romantic one, the latter usually falling into
the "suffer-and-die-together" category.

But it is precisely this, his refusal of *togetherness*, that gives
Antonioni his power. We have already had occasion to say this,
and we repeat it here, with a reference from Pavese: "Love has
the peculiar virtue of stripping the lovers naked, not before one
another, but each before himself." It is just here, in this feeling of
being naked before oneself, that the trap of solitude springs on
Antonioni's lovers. There is no salvation; afterwards, they will be
able to do only two things: separate or destroy one another. Love
will remain always the temporary comfort in, but never the reason
or the justification for, life.

The Poet of Matriarchy

DOMINIQUE FERNANDEZ
[From *La Nouvelle Revue Française*, November 1960]

In *L'Avventura* we have Antonioni's universe set up and in position. It resembles—this we must admit—those of all the great
modern creative artists. On the subject of the unsuccessful artist,
on the impossible couple, on the vanity of life's quest, on the in-
evitability of solitude—on none of these is Antonioni really original.
There is, of course, the splendor of his images; but Moravia, in
Lo Sdegno, and Rossellini, in *Viaggio in Italia,* had already developed the theme of a beauty which not only serves no good purpose
but even works harm.

It seems to me that however commonplace Antonioni's original
idea for *L'Avventura* may have been, he was led somewhere along
the way to abandon it entirely and to discover, in the failure of
the Claudia-Sandro match, something quite distinct from the laws
that govern the impossibility of love. This impossibility, which we
find presented as an absolute by all modern artists, has become a
cliché, a myth and a bit of mystification as false as the romantic
mystification of the "triumph of love." Antonioni puts his finger on
a truth of a far more interesting order: in the relationships be-

tween men and women within contemporary society, and particularly in Italian society, the roles have been reversed. The man has abdicated from all responsibility, from all initiative, and it is the woman who has to choose both for herself and for him. . . .

Antonioni exalts matriarchy, the only form of society remaining today since men's surrender of their traditional role. He exalts it or he deplores it. . . . One point is clear in any case: it is false to speak of a metaphysical inability to communicate between human beings. The whole of the drama of modern life derives from the absurdity of the way tasks are divided between the sexes. The man no longer plays his role as man; the woman is forced to become hard and to lose her femininity. The couple no longer exists, because the partners no longer exist.

Antonioni gives a faithful account of what goes on in Italy, at least so far as the man—whom he describes with strict realism—is concerned. His vision of the woman is doubtless more subjective, more poetic—even if it is true that it is becoming easier and easier to find women in Milan or Rome who are cold and independent, who prefer their work, their solitude, their slow process of desiccation to a relationship that might diminish their stature. Antonioni, who derives from Baudelaire (*"la froide majesté de la femme stérile"*) and from Pavese, is the poet of Woman, of the society of women proud of their indulgence in a mutual, austere, and silent self-worship. Handling a piece of clothing together becomes a ceremony more important than love itself . . . watching a sea horizon side by side . . . competing for a man, yes, but fleeing a bilateral masculine relationship from which the solitary, accessory third party would necessarily be excluded.

As a criticism of Italian society, *L'Avventura* goes infinitely deeper and gives a far more accurate picture than does *La Dolce Vita*, that all-star stage show based on the latest scandal sheets. Antonioni is the only one who has revealed the real scandal—this reversal in the roles played by the two sexes, and the consequences for both sides. It would be interesting to know to what causes he attributes it. The statements he has made to the press on the archaic state of our civilization remain vague and confused. One wonders in particular how much blame he imputes to Catholicism, to the Vatican. Not a word is said on this subject in the film, apart from a parade of little seminarians kept in military order by priests, black against the white stucco of the church.

There is a single note in *L'Avventura* that is less pessimistic: if the man-woman relationship is impossible today—from lack of men and lack of women—at least there remains the mother-son relationship. The woman is to be the mother, rather than the equal, of her lover. This childless matriarchy (there are never any children in Antonioni's films) thus recovers, in the compassion granted to mediocre males, its maternal vocation. This is the meaning of the last scene in *Le Amiche* between Nene and the painter; it is the meaning of the last, admirable image in *L'Avventura*. Sandro is sitting on a bench, weeping; Claudia approaches him from behind, and standing (still standing), her eyes dry, she slowly passes her hand through his hair. That is all. She concedes that her love can exist only in pity for the loved object. She clings to the only wisdom possible, the wisdom that consists in recognizing the weakness of what she has found. She makes the only gift it is permitted to her to make, that of pardoning what she scorns. From now on, she must either coddle Sandro or lose him. There is no other possible outcome. The sun moves on its course, and soon a radiant sky will unfurl over Taormina.

Literary Cinema

GUIDO ARISTARCO
[From *Cinema Nuovo*, January–February 1961]

In speaking of a "literary cinema," particularly with reference to Antonioni, the term should not be understood in a restrictive sense but as indicating the director's ability to achieve the dignity of the writer, to equal his complexity and his subtleties. On this point we may recall Eisenstein's "intellectual cinema," his theory of the interior monologue, and Bresson's idea of the cinema as a kind of handwriting, a "camera style."

Let us leave aside for the moment the similarities which exist between Antonioni and Pavese. Another literary link is much more relevant: to Flaubert. No doubt Flaubert, not Balzac or Stendhal or Tolstoy, is for Antonioni the true summit of the nineteenth-century novel. In our own century his preference is obviously for Gide, Proust, Joyce, the "new novel" of France, rather than for Mann.

Following in the wake of Flaubert, Antonioni does not seem even to understand those who carry on the tradition of critical realism; he rejects any unnecessary dialectical devices for the formation of "characters"; he renounces (or appears to renounce) any stated thesis, any indirect intervention in the flow of events and any direct interpretation of the facts. He neither shares in nor recounts, but observes and describes, the flat, monotonous flow of everyday life. His novelistic universe is not composed, like Visconti's, of a dramatic progression of events. For this he substitutes a series of independent scenes in which time is the protagonist, both as the element which determines and sets in motion the characters and as the principle which annihilates them, swallows them up. We are slowly consumed by time, along with our hopes and ambitions: this is the saddest reality. This gradual, almost imperceptible langour, which quietly undermines life without producing the upheaval of a great catastrophe, is the experience on which Flaubert's *L'Éducation Sentimentale* rests. As, one might add, does the whole of the modern novel.

Such an idea of life and art is the point from which Antonioni sets out on the journey which will bring him to Camus' *L'Étranger*, to Robert Musil's *Man Without Qualities*, to Hermann Broch's *The Sleepwalkers*. It is not by chance that Valentina, in *La Notte*, is first shown to us reading Broch's book amidst that parade of possessed souls, the party guests at Brianza's villa—a parade which compares with the final party at the San Domenico Palace in Taormina, in *L'Avventura*.

From the point of view of style and structure, *La Notte* accentuates the static character of *L'Avventura*. Like the advanced modern novelists, Antonioni, after giving up plot, has today reached the point where he has still more definitely given up the convention of the protagonist and has succeeded in "de-heroicizing" his story. In *L'Avventura* we have already seen the advent of a kind of setting which almost dominates the film: "I felt the need to break up the action to a very high degree, by inserting scenes of a truly documentary character (a waterspout, the sea, the shark swimming by, etc.), but which, in fact, are indispensable to my purpose, because they serve the idea of the film." The movement of thoughts and mental associations instead of the movement of events, the ebb and flow of consciousness instead of individual heros, the simultaneity of different states of the soul, all these lie at the heart of *La Notte*. How are we to regard Lidia's interminable wandering, first through the chaos of urban life, then through the apparent tranquility of the suburb, if not as a long, continuous interior monologue, as the kaleidoscopic image of a disintegrating world that looms up within herself? And have we not already been given an equally beautiful example of the interior monologue in Claudia's awakening in the luxury hotel bedroom in Taormina? In *La Notte*, as in *L'Avventura*, Antonioni displays the maturity he has achieved in this sort of analysis; here lies the novelty of his cinematographic language.

From the "intellectual cinema" of Eisenstein and his theory of the "interior monologue" based on Joyce, the psychological cinema, in the new meaning of the term—according to which the whole of reality is identified with the content of consciousness, and things acquire meaning only insofar as they form part of a psychic experience—has climbed to its greatest heights, surpassing Bresson's successes and even the best of Bergman. In Chaplin, in Visconti, working as they do from psychology as it was conceived in the nineteenth-century novel, "the soul and the character stand opposed to the world and the real, like positive and negative poles, and psychology is nothing more than the antithetical relationship between the subject and the object, the *I* and the *not-I*, the interior and the exterior worlds." In Antonioni, on the contrary, as in the literature of the new century, the problem consists less in characterizing the individual personality than in making a precise analysis of the psychic machinery itself.

A New Feeling for Reality

ALBERTO MORAVIA

[From *L'Espresso*, Rome, February 26, 1961]

Most Italian films, if they were translated into literary works, would turn out to be romantic tear-jerkers for young ladies, crime fiction or, at best, stories in the nineteenth-century tradition. Antonioni is one of the very few directors whose films, if rendered into prose, would not cut a sorry figure beside the most sophisticated products of modern narrative literature.

Some observers have spoken, in reference to *La Notte*, of a new cinematographic language. This is partly correct, but before speaking of language one must speak of a new approach to reality, from which that language derives. This applies to all the arts, including the cinema.

The feeling for reality expressed in Antonioni's works does indeed constitute something new in Italian cinema. Our directors are usually and primarily concerned with describing objects and setting them in motion. The substance of their art is naturalistic and dramatic. Antonioni, however, is preoccupied with making us know things and people rather than with describing them, more intent on furnishing concrete examples of people's inner feelings than on making them perform for us. Hence the complete elimination of everything that produces movement, incident, conflict, progression or agitation, such as psychology, plot development, characters and ideas.

Antonioni's reality is static, inert, visual—circumstantial, one might say. Anguish is the only feeling it inspires, and it is the feeling in which that reality is reflected, as in a mirror. Why this anguish? Because for Antonioni, reality seems absurd—that is, composed of objects bound together by no rationally perceptible links. Like a dream, or a totally foreign world.

For these reasons, the contemplation of a wall carries more weight than a carefully worked out dramatic action. In the first case, the character discovers something which halts him, opposes him, presents itself to him as a solid object; in the second, he will slip and lose his way among narrative conventions and psychological mechanisms. For example, when the writer's wife in *La Notte*, during her wanderings through Milan, stops before a wall and pulls a bit of plaster off it with her hand, we feel that this is the high point of the film—because at that moment the character is oppressed by a nameless, formless anguish, which Antonioni has expressed with a perfect image. By comparison, the Teddy boys' fight in the same film, although viewed through the same anguish, is still too dramatic and too "human." The expression of anguish does not require men, but it does need things—or, to phrase it differently, men reduced to the condition of things.

Someone might ask at this point whether anguish and the other emotions that border on it do not lie outside the ordinary range of feeling, and whether they are not therefore of little significance. In other words, whether Antonioni does not run the risk of falling over the edge into the exceptional and the pathological. Let us answer at once: exactly the opposite is true. A day in the life of any human being is, in fact, almost always a dark chaos from which emerge—if they do emerge—only rare moments of conscious, motivated action. We spend most of our lives pulling bits of plaster off walls—in other words, contemplating reality without either entering into or understanding it. This is a perfectly normal condition, which leads many people to passivity, to resignation, to something like complacent hedonism. But sometimes, as with Antonioni's characters, the refusal to accept this condition, with its absence of communication and its automatism, leads to anguish.

The objector may still ask why such situations, marked as they are by the feeling of anguish, have only recently attracted the attention of artists. Why have we until so recently always been shown characters engaged in action, dramatically involved? The answer is that attention has shifted as the result of a change in values. Formerly, importance was given only to the rare moments of conscious and reasoned action in each human day, and the chaos from which they emerged was passed over in silence. Today the contrary is true. This transformation is due to the profound crisis that has led us to question the motives which guide our actions. Between an action which is profitable, but false, and a contemplation which is anguished, but lucid, it is clear now that the second is preferable.

A new feeling for reality naturally gives rise to new forms of expression. Antonioni has brought to the screen, perhaps for the first time in Italy, methods and images which belong to the modern novel and poetry. Certain sequences in *La Notte* have caused a large part of the narrative and neorealistic cinema to grow old before our eyes. We believe that this is the greatest tribute that could be paid Antonioni.

Antonioni and Music

GIOVANNI FUSCO

The first rule for any musician who intends to collaborate with Antonioni is to forget that he is a musician. This is the fruit of my experience as composer of the music for all his feature films up to *La Notte*, for which, in the end, no music at all was written.

A peculiar and very personal relationship exists between Antonioni and music: he hates it, and he cannot do without it. But we ought not to conclude that this derives from an attitude lightly arrived at; the revulsion he feels toward music is the fruit of long meditation. His sole and true obsession is the cinema. The translation of life into the exact dimensions of the cinema, the search for cinematographic equivalents to human values: this is what matters to him.

To what point does music participate in this search? Or, to put it better: What is the role of music in the cinema? The problem is, of course, not a new one; what is new, so it seems to me, is the solution we have found to it.

It is unnecessary to say that I personally detest films overflowing with useless, assertive music. Nor do I consider valid the type of background music that Cocteau once defined as "furniture music," a kind of hum in which one tone is as good as another, and the whole score ends by "soiling" the poetic atmosphere of the work. On the contrary, I believe that if music is to be regularly included in a film it ought to perform its own function: that of musically illuminating certain situations, of contributing *from a distance* to the work's dramatic texture and thus help the spectator to understand it at its most secret levels, and particularly to plumb the depths of the characters.

In order to attain these ends, the music must necessarily be incisive and rather spaced out. The most effective results can be obtained with the smallest orchestras. When I am working with a director of Antonioni's stature, I eliminate the orchestra entirely. I have been using small bands for many years now: a few instruments are often all that is necessary. In *Hiroshima, Mon Amour,* I used a relatively large band: nine instruments. In *I Vinti,* I made do with one piano. And in *Cronaca di un Amore,* I feel I gave the best possible demonstration of my convictions concerning cinematographic music: I used only a saxophone, and the solo was executed in masterly style by Georges Mûle of the Paris Conservatory. Indeed, with *Cronaca di un Amore,* I felt that I had reached the point of transforming the music into a skeleton of itself. But Antonioni would like to go still further: to abolish music from films altogether, or else to accept it only when it is required by the situation. A character enters a concert hall, or we see people dancing or a beggar playing a street-organ: these are the kinds of music that Antonioni is willing to tolerate in the cinema. The other kind —the kind I compose for him—drives him into a state of extreme nervousness.

When he tackles the problem of the musical instruments, he is *already prejudiced* against what they are going to play. During the sound-track recording session, he takes his place in the technician's glass cage, but the musicians have not even finished playing the first measures before he has begun to buzz the intercom; in our section of the room, we hear his voice, irritated and pained at the same time: "Giovanni, can't we do without that instrument?" Or else: "This bit? Let's cut it." And then he shuts off the intercom.

Antonioni has also supervised the music as it was being composed, sitting next to me at the piano, calling for endless encores, questioning everything, always discontented, always disconsolate, always worried. I must admit that he is not always easy to work with. He is a man of broad and excellent general culture (he studied music himself and there was a time when he even played the violin); he is dominated by eternal doubts, as are all people in whom the intellectual faculties predominate. Intelligence is the natural state of his being: an intelligence that might be described as cutting and that, in the end, shuts him off in a profound solitude. It sometimes seems to me that he has to make a real effort to listen to the person speaking to him. I have often heard myself pleading, almost with bitterness, to save pieces that I composed in the very spirit of his own poetic mood. Perhaps he was the one who was right; but it cost me a great deal to give in. On the other hand, I am sure that I have succeeded in leading him into certain areas and making him accept them, *musically*, without his realizing it.

Despite the problems, our collaboration has always worked out for the best. A process of osmosis takes place between Antonioni and myself. This process lies behind the success of our efforts in a number of works where the music preserves intact its proper function.

On *L'Avventura*

WILLIAM S. PECHTER
[From an article in *The Kenyon Review*, Spring 1962]

L'Avventura has been hailed as the greatest existent example of "the *cinéma pur*," a film existing absolutely, without reference to any meaning; and at the festival at Cannes where it was jeered and hooted, *L'Avventura* won a special prize for something like (and I quote from memory) "the unusual beauty of its images in its development of a new cinematic language." Both responses, in their way, affirm the first principle of film unappreciation: when you don't know what it all means, praise its photography. And yet the film is manifestly neither without conscious, deliberate meaning, nor new, in any experimental sense; certainly, it is one of the films I would wish least to single out for the beauty of its imagery, that imagery, beautiful as it is, being so inseparably allied to the film's meaning. What is new in *L'Avventura* is not the language but the voice; the voice of an artist in absolute control of his medium, and in pursuit of meaning; and this in the medium which most lends itself to the illusion of its impersonal, creative autonomy, its independence of any individual artist. That this voice and the imagination which informs it are so fundamentally, so traditionally, novelistic ones is what is unusual, and what is extraordinary is the extent to which the medium responds to such a voice and imagination. *L'Avventura* has been called an abstract film, yet it abounds with concrete, realistic observation. The love affair between Claudia and Sandro, for example, obviously regarded by Antonioni as a moral failure, is nevertheless depicted with great fidelity to the detail of its natural development, even with humor and charm. But *L'Avventura* does move always from its accumulation of particular, often fragmentary, detail toward some integrity of abstract idea, some general truth; it is the movement, I maintain, despite the critical vogue of "concrete detail," of every true novel, from *Don Quixote* to *The Victim*.

To the extent that Antonioni's imagination is novelistic, he sees all his characters in their individual differences. He is without contempt for even the most contemptible of his characters. Like Dickens, he seems to love even his "villains," although, unlike Dickens, he has no villains, only cripples. But to the extent that Antonioni's imagination is a moral one, and this moral imagination is, I think, his defining quality as an artist, he sees all his characters as the same, lost in their similarity. The self-conscious cynics and sybarites are, finally, not much different from the "decent" few who gather about their fringe; the whore, finally, not dissimilar to the lover; the initially confident, nonchalant Sandro and the initially lively, independent Claudia end alike in their shared, mutual weakness. All are united in this common weakness, all made anonymous, *manqué;* all missing persons. Weakness, for Antonioni, is not the grounds for some final surge of redemptive compassion, for forgiveness, but the mark of culpability, of moral failure. For we might be strong, we might be responsible. Claudia, acquiescing to Sandro, abdicates her self. Antonioni's meaning, clearly but complexly, is the loss of self in a society preoccupied with self. And one can only marvel at the utter rightness of the action, the sustained metaphor, he has invented to embody and contain this meaning.

An Artist for an Age

STANLEY KAUFFMANN
[Excerpted from *The New Republic*, February 26, 1962]

. . . Antonioni is achieving what many contemporary artists in his and other fields are seeking, and not often with his success: renewal of his art rather than repetition. He seems to be making the miracle: finding a way to speak to us about ourselves today without crankily throwing away all that went before and without being bound by it. He is reshaping the idea of the content of film drama, discarding ancient and less ancient concepts, redirecting traditional audience expectations toward immersion in character rather than conflict of character. He is reshaping time itself in his films, taking it out of its customary synoptic form, wringing intensity out of its distention, daring to ask us to "live through" experiences with less distillation, deriving his drama from the very texture of such experiences and their juxtaposition, rather than from formal clash and climax and resolution. Fundamentally, he gives us characters whose drama consists in facing life minute after minute rather than in moving through organized plots with articulated obstacles; who have no well-marked cosmos to use as a tennis player uses a court; who live and die without the implication of a divine eye that sees their virtues (whether men do or not) and cherishes them.

John Grierson once said that when a director dies he becomes a photographer; but Antonioni gets emotional utility—in a film about *people*—out of surfaces and compositions. He uses photography for enrichment, not for salon gasps: for example, the scene in *La Notte* where Lidia goes for a ride in the rain with a man and the downpour seems to put the car in danger of dissolution.

The sequence in *La Notte* that best represents Antonioni's style is the one in which Lidia slips away from the publisher's party and wanders through the streets. Conditioned as we are, we *expect* something; we think she is off to meet a lover, or to kill herself, or to get involved in an accident. But nothing happens; and everything happens. She strolls past a bus conductor eating a sandwich and is fascinated by his existence and his appetite in the same universe with her; she passes two men laughing uproariously at a joke and she smiles, too, although she has not heard it, anxious to join them, to be one of the human race; she encounters a crying child and kneels briefly and unsuccessfully to comfort it; she tears a flake of rust off a corroding wall; she sees two young men punching each other ferociously, watches, horrified, then screams for them to stop. (The victor thinks she must be attracted to him and starts to pursue her, and so Antonioni touches another old tribal nerve.) Then in the suburbs she watches some boys shooting off rockets. She finds she is in a neighborhood where she and Giovanni used to come years before. She telephones him and he drives out to pick her up.

By drama-school definition, it is not a cumulative dramatic sequence. It is a miniature recapitulation, deftly done, of the possibilities of life: a child and an old woman, a man eating and a man punching, sunlight on a fountain and a greasy, lewd stall-keeper. Antonioni holds it all together with something like the surface tension of liquids and, by not commenting, comments. It is essentially as drastic a revolution as abstract-expressionist painting or Beckett's litany-like dialogue, but Antonioni has not estranged us in order to speak to us about loneliness; he has not sacrificed the link of recognition to make new images; he has not had to use absurdity to convey the absurd.

Of every directorial technique he is an easy master. I specify only two. His use of sound: the low-pitched conversation in the hospital is interrupted by the passage of a helicopter like a pause in music so that the hushed key will not become tedious. His symbolism (which is unobtrusive): the mushroom cloud of smoke that envelops the boy who fires the rocket, and the fact that Giovanni meets Lidia after her walk in front of a long-abandoned church.

For me, Antonioni has made in *La Notte* and in *L'Avventura* the most subtly truthful theatrical works about the relation of the sexes since Joyce's *Exiles*. But he has done more. In *La Notte* he has used a vitiated marriage as a metaphor of the crisis of faith in our age, the faith within which profoundest love and pettiest whim have always been contained. He has used his camera as a hound of non-heaven ranging through the streets of Milan to find the beauty in necessity, the assurance in knowing that one can live without assurances. This film leaves us less deceived; thus, with the truth in us less encumbered.

Antonioni's *La Notte*: Dissolution of Love

JAMES STOLLER
[Excerpted from *The Supplement, Columbia Daily Spectator,*
April 20, 1962]

. . . As befits the title, *La Notte* offers us a darker, heavier world than *L'Avventura;* the strokes, too, are heavier—to the point, some will say, of obviousness. It's true that the symbolism tends to grow leaden and insistent, and points are underlined too overtly. Coming upon a row of fireplugs, Lidia (Jeanne Moreau) fondles one longingly, in the silliest kind of now-why-can't-my-husband-be-like-that? gesture. And when she phones her husband to tell him how much he'd like the rockets, I thought of a friend's used copy of *The Waste Land* in which someone had circled "cock" and written "symbol of fertility" in the margin.

Still, it is perhaps in its audacity, its outrageousness, that *La Notte* is strongest: in the dares it takes and the beauty it manages to develop in the face of concepts no more promising than alienation, paralysis, death in life. In Joyce's *Dubliners,* the people broke out of their paralysis into moments of transcendent remorse or regret. Here the cards are stacked, and the wife remembers not Michael Furey but a selfless love that stifled her. Absolutely nothing in the film, no memory or event, works as a model, a point worth aspiring to. . . .

Then there is the long party sequence, which does not look to me like its director's work. For lengthy stretches it is lax, uninterestingly photographed, sloppily paced; it does not have that air of calm improbability that we associate with Antonioni—so much does it not that I am tempted to suspect him of muddying it deliberately, to accentuate the boredom. For with what grace he pulls the loose threads together at the end! Yet that end is itself a kind of dare; Giovanni's failure to recognize his own letter is beauti-

"…the cards are stacked…" Jeanne Moreau as Lidia, with Antonioni during production of *La Notte*. "…his camera…a hound of non-heaven…" From *La Notte*.

fully outrageous, and asking us to accept the obviousness of the gimmick taxes our tolerance as much as asking us to believe he would have forgotten it taxes our credulity. . . .

Another "dare," I think, is the montage sequence in which Lidia, tired of the cocktail party, wanders about Milan. Geoffrey Nowell-Smith in *Sight and Sound* (Winter, 1961-62) found it "an evaluative montage of great precision and beauty." For me, however, there was something stiff and academic to it, the way there almost always is when discontinuous cutting is used to develop a series of explicit, one-to-one meanings (as in Eisenstein) rather than (as in *Breathless*) for the sake of suggestiveness or sweep. Now, assuming my feeling was valid, I'd think Antonioni too much a master of cutting rhythms to have provoked it undeliberately. You always know his dissonances are there because he wanted them. . . .

I've been too much, I think, on the defensive. At the same time, perhaps I have not been altogether honest, for all my respect and fascination do not enable me to maintain with a clear conscience that I found *La Notte* a fully satisfying experience—satisfying in the way that films like *The Rules of the Game, Pather Panchali,* and even *Breathless,* are satisfying. Might I with some justification speak of a kind of minimal contact point in one's relation to a work of art? In a film of contemporary life to which I might be able to latch on as I can latch on only barely to *La Notte,* I would want some grappling with the fact of interaction between persons—with love, with loss, with friction, too. Not more than this but—if the work is to seem useful—certainly not less. Antonioni consciously limits his canvas and offers less. I won't criticize his card-stacking, for it is essential to his vision; but I am forced, I think, to limit my engagement.

La Notte is not the film of a young man, and perhaps by forty-five one grows exhausted and disenchanted, and the sad, repetitious patterns of love and strife by which people define themselves with respect to one another cease to have much interest. When I imagine how a man might arrive at that point, I feel I have no business complaining; when, on the other hand, I remember Yeats writing at seventy of lust and vanity and disgrace, I am certain that I had better run the risk of being called unknowing, and ask of films what for me is real. I am finally saying, then, that *La Notte*

—moving though it is—has very little, now, to say to me, and incidentally that it is thereby like too many other films. . . .

On Antonioni's *L'Eclisse*

INGMAR BERGMAN
[Excerpted from *Stockholms-Tidningen* October 25, 1962]

I am truly impressed by the uncompromising self-confession to which Antonioni is so deeply committed. Within the film industry (which must be considered a "heavy" industry), Antonioni's contribution is both new and fresh and of enduring value.

What seems strange to me, however, is his limited interest in his actors, in their instruction and guidance. Therefore *La Notte* was a greater experience for me than *L'Eclisse*, because Jeanne Moreau is a brilliant actress, which cannot quite be said of the very talented but technically insecure Monica Vitti.

To me, the actor is and always will be the most eloquent means of presenting the visions of a film creator.

Eclipse: Silence Is Content

JONAS MEKAS
[Excerpted from *The Village Voice*, December 13, 1962]

You have heard much about the silence in Antonioni's films, particularly in *La Notte*. *Eclipse* is still more silent. There is a gradual disappearance of dialogue from *L'Avventura* to *Eclipse*. So they say Antonioni rediscovered silent cinema, he is going back to the true principles of cinema. They look at it formalistically. But Antonioni's silence has nothing to do with principles of cinema: Antonioni's silence comes from his content, is part of his content, or, simply, *is* his content. His people become more and more silent as the trilogy progresses, as the introspection of the characters increases. They haven't lost communication. Antonioni's films aren't about communication, as all critics have conspired to insist. His films are about people, about *us*, who don't have anything to communicate, who don't feel a need to communicate, whose human essence is dying. Antonioni's films are about the death of the human soul.

At the end of Antonioni's trilogy, people stare into each other and their surroundings, and the surroundings and the objects stare back at them, with a cold, unmerciful eye. Man and objects have become equals—it is a terrifying state for man, but that's where he is, and that's what Antonioni says. The image of man in 1962 presented in this film of breathtaking visual beauty is a fearful lunatic silence of a trapped animal, of a man at the dead end, the time when man looks to the heavens for signs of change: he can't continue as he is.

I knew what Antonioni would make after *La Notte*. I don't know what he will make after *Eclipse*. There is no way back for Antonioni, and the solutions for man have not yet been revealed.

Artist at Work

STANLEY KAUFFMANN
[Excerpted from *The New Republic*, December 29, 1962]

Although *Eclipse* is as consistently interesting as the other two films in the trilogy, it is not nearly as moving. I think this is because Vittoria is more a symbol than a person—almost a pageant-figure, the Spirit of the Modern Girl. Her uncertainties and frustrations seem selected to represent a social group, rather than to create *her*. A large part of the reason for this—the sense that she is a compilation of recognizable problems rather than a person in her own right—is that we get from Vittoria no feeling of individual motion. We have no idea of the possibilities from which uncertainties have kept her. She is not even a bona fide floater. All we know about her nonsex life is that she does translations. (Does this pay her considerable rent and clothes bill?) The architect in *L'Avventura*, the novelist in *The Night*, were men whose possibly fruitful and happy lives, we could see, were harrowed up and thwarted. We are asked to feel much the same about Vittoria but without the same basis. I am not saying that she ought to be a frustrated artist or intellectual. But if we could sense that there was *something* she wanted in life to which contemporary malaise was

"...their permanent 'availability' but also their predestination to solitude..." Alain Delon (Piero) and Monica Vitti (Vittoria) at different stages in *L'Eclisse*.

an impediment—even if it was only to be a happy floater—it would deepen her shadows, make her a woman. Her context and presentation are so beautiful that we must be interested in her, but the sadness of the earlier films—of an *individual's* condition—is missing.

Monica Vitti does her best with the role, which is a great deal. She has *sagesse,* humor, sensitivity. But she lacks the materials she was given previously: the fascinated horror of the girl in *L'Avventura* watching herself fall into the arms of the lover of a friend so lately presumed dead; the precocious maturity of the rich girl in *The Night* who sees herself being used as an emotional refuge by an older couple. Here she has little character.

Piero is inevitably more vivid because he is enormously active in a job he enjoys, and is not coarsened by it. He resembles the hero of Walker Percy's novel, *The Moviegoer*—also a stockbroker—who says:

> "Money is a good counterpoise to beauty. Beauty, the quest of beauty alone, is a whoredom. Ten years ago I pursued beauty and gave no thought to money. I listened to the lovely tunes of Mahler and felt a sickness in my very soul. Now I pursue money and on the whole feel better."

. . . Antonioni now has such mastery of the vocabulary of film that he can violate rules to his purpose. For example, there are no dissolves in *Eclipse,* yet there is no choppiness of transition; the miraculously keen editing makes time his servant. One feels in Antonioni's work, as one rarely does in any art, that he has said exactly what he wants to say exactly as he wants to say it.

But if there is not a flabby or false moment, *Eclipse* has none of the overpowering emotional quality of the previous two films. And, undeniably, it has some visual effects reminiscent of those films—like the heads seen against stark white walls. Whether these repetitions are design or limitation it is not yet possible to say. In a real sense, we won't know all about *Eclipse* until we see Antonioni's future work. Meanwhile, although I cannot claim the enthusiasm for this picture that I have felt for its two predecessors, it is a happiness to know that, in the muddled, half-strangulated world of film, a powerful and pure artist continues to work.

Eclipse: Man Into Object

JOHN SIMON
[Excerpted from *The New Leader,* February 4, 1963]

Eclipse is a metaphor made up of many smaller metaphors. Man is in eclipse because he has lost belief, without which he becomes an object. And not content with making himself into a thing, man must also debase things, remove them further from reality or purpose. But things will have their vengeance; they may, in fact, supplant us.

Take the first shot of the film. A nondescript white object lies on top of a row of books. The books are in sharp focus, the object is only a blob. Presently it moves, and is revealed to be a man's white-sleeved elbow. Later on, the heroine remarks, "There are days when a chair, a table, a book, or a man are all the same thing to me." Our first glimpse of Vittoria shows her framing some objects with an empty frame, to make them back out of reality into a pseudopicture. And the walls are covered with action paintings in which both man and object are traduced to the absurd.

Throughout the film, Antonioni exhibits his customary brilliance in handling details. There is the moment when Vittoria decides to go to Piero's apartment and give herself to him, only to be struck motionless in the middle of the street as she watches another young man, handsome in a very different way, walk by. "He has a beautiful face!" she exclaims with the wistfulness of a sudden, aching insight into a world where one is free to make choices, but condemned to choose. Or the moment when Piero tells Vittoria that he will kiss her on the other side of the street: The roadway is ribbed with thick white lines to denote a crossing, but these flat lines, beyond which lurks decision, become at once a steep, exhausting stairway. In the middle, Vittoria observes, "We are halfway across," reminding us, surely not accidentally, of Dante's first line.

Particularly imaginative is the last sequence of the film, from which the hero and heroine have faded away. The movie began with the end of a previous love affair, and now we realize that in its beginning was its end—that what seemed merely a point of departure was, in truth, a giant flash-forward hanging over the rest of the film and the rest of Vittoria's life. So we see now, for the last time, Vittoria and Piero embracing in his office. Suddenly, both look into the camera: His eyes show discomfiture and the need to escape to something else; hers, fear and despair. They make brave promises for the future. But the objects now take over. Piero is promptly surrounded by stock-exchange reports flapping in the breeze from the window, pencils hedging him in, and a whole orchestra of telephones from bass to piccolo clamoring for his attention. He yields almost contentedly. Vittoria wanders away alongside of curious parapets and fences isolating her anguished face from the world.

Forthwith we are at the place where these lovers used to meet. The customary objects and sounds are all there as before, living their ineluctable, unswerving and therefore real life; but the people are different, unknown to us, meaningless. A sports car we associate with the hero, the sliver of wood which the heroine dropped into a water container, the chattering burlap and straw covering on an unfinished building, the jet planes which strange eyes are watching, the white lines of the crossing which is nobody's *gradus ad Parnassum* now. Closeups of an embittered old man and a worn-looking woman: the hero and heroine as they will be?

The last and most awe-inspiring image of all: An ultramodern street light goes on; in blinding close-up, it takes over the screen; and the movie ends. Is this radiant end an eclipse? It is: the brilliance of artificial suns, the splendor of objects, and the long, neon-streaked night of the soul.

Why should so many superb details add up to an unsatisfactory film? Because we cannot care for people who will not even put up a fight against boredom, because we are not allowed to go inside the characters, because no possible alternative to defeat is offered. A young woman from Kenya arouses Vittoria's longing for Africa; but even in that unovercivilized land we hear of anxiety and bloody turmoil. There, too, life is becoming objectified—what was once an elephant's foot is now the leg of a coffee table; and objects overshadow the living—Kenya is at its best in the inanimate photographs in an album and on walls.

Eclipse is a luminous failure.

L'Eclisse: "a metaphor."

For L'Avventura: *Statement distributed at the 1960 Cannes Film Festival*

[Published by the *Bulletins du Festival de Cannes,* May 16, 1960]

Aware of the exceptional importance of Michelangelo Antonioni's film, *L'Avventura,* and appalled by the displays of hostility it has aroused, the undersigned critics and members of the profession are anxious to express their admiration for the maker of this film.

Convinced that they will be joined by others who share their enthusiasm, they invite them to make known their support.
Signed:

Roberto Rossellini
Mario Ruspoli di Poggio-Suasa
Jean Namur
Guillaume Hanoteau (*Paris-Match*)
René Gilson (*Cinema 60*)
Jean Barral
Janine André-Bazin
Alice Sapritch
Anatole Dauman (Argos Films)
Henry Magnan (*Paris-Jour*)
Pierre Marcabru (*Combat*)
Samuel Lachize (*L'Humanité*)
Nelly Kaplan
A.-S. Labarthe (*Radio-Cinéma*)
Jean-Pierre Barrot (*Télécinex*)
Jean Thuillier (*Les Editions Cinégraphiques*)
Ennio Lorenzini
Yvonne Decaris

Guy Allombert (*Image et Son*)
Jean Gaborit (*Les Grands Films Classiques*)
Albert Cervoni (*France Nouvelle*)
Émile Breton (*La Marseillaise*)
François Maurin (*L'Humanité-Dimanche*)
Meerhneche (the Polish press agency)
Talmon-Gros (general secretary of the German Associa-
    tion of Art Cinemas)
Philippe Lifchitz (Argos Films)
Pierre Billard (editor-in-chief of Cinema 60)
Maurice Ronet
Georges Sadoul
Jacqueline Michel (*Parisien Libéré*)
Gene Moskowicz (*Variety*)
Michel Aubriant
Jeander
Claude Mauriac (*Figaro Littéraire*)
Robert Benayoun (*Présence du Cinéma*)

This declaration was presented to Michelangelo Antonioni immediately after it was drawn up.

Filmography

I. IN COLLABORATION

As assistant director:

I DUE FOSCARI, directed by Enrico Fulchignoni (1942)

LES VISITEURS DU SOIR, directed by Marcel Carné (1942)

As co-scenarist:

I DUE FOSCARI, in collaboration with G. Campanile Mancini, Mino Doletti, Enrico Fulchignoni. Film directed by Enrico Fulchignoni (1942).

UN PILOTA RITORNA, in collaboration with Rosario Leone, Ugo Betti, Massimo Mida, Gherardo Gherardi. Film directed by Roberto Rossellini (1942).

CACCIA TRAGICA, in collaboration with Giuseppe de Santis, Carlo Lizzani, Cesare Zavattini, Corrado Alvaro, Umberto Barbaro, Tullio Pinelli. Film directed by Giuseppe de Santis (1947).

LO SCEICCO BIANCO, in collaboration with Federico Fellini and Tullio Pinelli. Film directed by Federico Fellini (1952).

II. AS DIRECTOR

Documentaries

GENTE DEL PO (1943-1947)

Photography: Piero Portalupi

Music: Mario Labroca

Production: I.C.E.T.-Carpi

The voyage of a barge down the Po. The villages along its banks and the men who live in them.

N.U. (NETTEZA URBANA) (1948)

Photography: Giovanni Ventimiglia

Music: Jazz arrangement by Giovanni Fusco and Prelude by J. S. Bach

Production: Lux Film

Winner of the Silver Ribbon (annual prize awarded by the Italian Guild of Film Journalists)

A typical working day of Roman street sweepers, beginning at dawn and continuing until they go home in the evening.

L'AMOROSA MENZOGNA (1948-1949)
Photography: Renato del Frate
Music: Giovanni Fusco
Production: Fortuna Film
Winner of the Silver Ribbon, 1949
   The life of actors for photographic comic books. The circumstances under which such books are produced and the peculiarities of their readers.

SUPERSTIZIONE (1948-1949)
Photography: Giovanni Ventimiglia
Music: Giovanni Fusco
Production: I.C.E.T.-Carpi
   Various forms of superstitution and magic as practiced today in a village in the Marches.

LA FUNIVIA DEL FALORIA (1950)
Photography: Goffredo Bellisario and Ghedina
Music: Teo Usuelli
Production: Teo Usuelli
   The overhead railway from Monte Faloria to Cortina d'Ampezzo.

SETTE CANNE UN VESTITO (1949)
Photography: Giovanni Ventimiglia
Music: stock
Production: I.C.E.T.
   The manufacture of rayon at Torviscosa, near Trieste.

LA VILLA DEI MOSTRI (1950)
Photography: Giovanni de Paoli
Music: Giovanni Fusco
Production: Filmus
   The statuary depicting monstrous human figures at the ancient Villa Orsini at Bomarzo, near Viterbo.

UOMINI IN PIU (1955)
Production: C.I.M.E. (The Intergovernmental Committee for European Migrations)
   The problem of overpopulation and emigration in Italy.

Feature Films

CRONACA DI UN AMORE (1950)
Story: Michelangelo Antonioni
Screenplay: Michelangelo Antonioni, Danièle d'Anza, Silvio Giovaninetti, Francesco Maselli, Piero Tellini
Photography: Enzo Serafin
Sets: Piero Filippone
Costumes (for Lucia Bose): Ferdinando Sarmi

Music: Giovanni Fusco

Actors: Lucia Bose (Paola), Massimo Girotti (Guido), Ferdinando Sarmi (Fontana), Gino Rossi, Marika Rowsky, Rosa Mirafiore, Rubi d'Alma

Production: Franco Villani and Stefano Caretta for Villani Films

Shooting: in and around Milan; studios

Premières: Rome, Nov. 25, 1950; Biarritz (Festival du Film Maudit), Oct., 1950; Paris, June 1, 1951

Winner of the Grand Prize for direction at the Punta del Este Festival, 1951

Winner of the Silver Ribbon, 1951

After several years of marriage, Fontana, a Milanese industrialist, orders a private investigation to be made into the past of his young wife, Paola. Paola, before her marriage, had had an affair with Guido, a poor young man whose fiancée was killed shortly afterwards in an elevator accident. The investigation uncovers these facts and reveals the possibility that the lovers may have been guilty of the girl's death.

Learning that the investigation is taking place, Guido sees Paola again. They begin their affair once more, despite her marriage and the difference in status that it has set up between them. They begin to think about doing away with the husband. Guido refuses. Paola insists. One evening Guido goes to a spot where Fontana passes every day in his car. A little farther down the road, the car crashes. Fontana is killed. An accident? Suicide? No one will ever know, but the death they had so much wished for opens up a gap between the lovers which separates them forever. Guido departs Milan, leaving Paola alone.

I VINTI (1952)

Screenplay: Michelangelo Antonioni, Suso Cecchi d'Amico, Diego Fabbri, Turi Vasile

Photography: Enzo Serafin

Sets: Gianni Polidori

Music: Giovanni Fusco

Actors:

Italian Episode: Anna Maria Ferrero, Franco Interlenghi, Eduardo Cianelli, Evi Maltagliati, Umberto Sparado, Gastone Renzelli

English Episode: Peter Reynolds, Patrick Barr, Fay Compton, Eileen Moore

French Episode: Henry Poirier, André Jacques, Jean-Pierre Mocky, Etchika Choureau, Annie Noël

Production: Film-Constellazione, S.G.C.

Shooting: Rome, London, Paris

Première: The Venice Festival (out of competition), Sept. 4, 1953

Three separate episodes dealing with the crimes of post-war adolescents. Adapted from authentic stories.

English Episode: A young man commits a crime in order to get himself talked about.

Italian Episode: A middle-class youth gets involved with a gang of dope peddlers. He is killed by the police while trying to escape.

French Episode: During an outing in the country, a group of juvenile delinquents kill one of their comrades.

LA SIGNORA SENZA CAMELIE (1952-1953)

Story: Michelangelo Antonioni

Screenplay: Michelangelo Antonioni, Suso Cecchi d'Amico, Francesco Maselli, P. M. Pasinetti

Photography: Enzo Serafin

Sets: Gianni Polidori

Music: Giovanni Fusco

Actors: Lucia Bose, Andrea Cecchi, Gino Cervi, Ivan Desny, Alain Cuny, Monica Clay, Anna Carena, Enrico Glori

Production: Domenico Forges Davanzati for E.N.I.C.

Shooting: Rome, Venice, Milan

Premières: Rome, Feb. 27, 1953; Paris, Sept. 13, 1960

First spotted in Milan, where she had been a shopgirl, Clara Manni has become the star of a number of cheap, sexy films. With the consent of her parents—who are delighted with the unexpected increase in their fortunes—but against her own will, she is married to her producer. After their marriage, he becomes jealous and forbids her to continue her career in the erotic roles that have brought her success. Clara grows bored. Despite the friendly warnings of her former director, she feels she is capable of playing a great role, that of Joan of Arc. This ambitious production, on which her husband risks his fortune, is a disastrous failure at Venice.

Distressed, Clara hopes to regain her happiness with a young diplomat, for whom, however, she represents nothing more than a passing adventure. Her husband, cornered and on the edge of bankruptcy, attempts suicide. Clara goes back to work on a very bad film in an attempt to help get him back on his feet; then she divorces him.

Everything has tumbled down around her and Clara,

empty, lost, returns to her second-rate existence as a commercial star.

TENTATO SUICIDIO—An episode in the film *L'Amore in Città* (1953)

Photography: Gianni di Venanzo
Sets: Gianni Polidori
Music: Mario Nascimbene
Actors: The survivors of the events recorded in the film
Production: Faro Film
Shooting: Rome
Premières: Rome, Nov. 27, 1953; Paris, Feb. 8, 1957

Survivors of suicide attempts are questioned by the investigator; they recount and re-enact their attempts before the camera.

LE AMICHE (1955)

Story: adapted by Michelangelo Antonioni from Cesare Pavese's *Tra Donne Sole*
Screenplay: Michelangelo Antonioni, Suso Cecchi d'Amico, Alba de Cespedes
Photography: Gianni di Venanzo
Sets: Gianni Polidori
Music: Giovanni Fusco
Actors: Eleonora Rossi Drago, Valentina Cortese, Gabriele Ferzetti, Franco Fabrizi, Ettore Manni, Madeleine Fischer, Yvonne Furneaux, Anna Maria Pancani
Production: Trionfalcine
Shooting: Turin
Premières: Venice, Sept. 7, 1955; Rome, Nov. 18, 1955; Paris, Sept. 6, 1957
Prizes: Silver Lion at the Venice Festival, 1955; Grolla d'oro, 1955; Nastro d'argento, 1955; Stella d'oro, 1959 (in Argentina)

Clelia, a young woman from Rome, comes to Turin to set up the local branch of a large fashion house. She becomes involved with a small group of idle and futile young women. Momina, who is separated from her husband, excels at the arts of trifling with men's affections and manipulating the affairs of her "friends." One of them, Rosetta, has already attempted to commit suicide. She becomes the mistress of Lorenzo, a painter who lives with the female potter Nene. When he learns that Nene wants to leave him, he brutally breaks with Rosetta. The girl makes a new suicide attempt and this time kills herself.

During the showing of the fashion collection, Clelia suddenly spills out her contempt for Momina, whom she accuses of being responsible for Rosetta's death. Then she breaks entirely with this corrupt circle and returns to Rome, at the same time abandoning a young factory foreman whom she thought she loved, but whose working-class status could never match her own position or fulfill her ambitions.

IL GRIDO (1957)

Story: Michelangelo Antonioni

Screenplay: Michelangelo Antonioni, Elio Bartolini, Ennio de Concini

Photography: Gianni di Venanzo

Sets: Franco Fontana

Costumes: Pia Marchesi

Music: Giovanni Fusco

Actors: Steve Cochran (Aldo), Alida Valli (Irma), Dorian Gray (Virginia), Betsy Blair (Elvia), Lynn Shaw (Andreina), Gabriella Pallotto, Gaetano Matteucci, Guerrino Campanili, Pina Boldrini

Production: Franco Cancellieri for S.P.A. Cinematografica, in collaboration with Robert Alexander Productions of New York

U.S. distributor: Astor Pictures

Shooting: The lower Po valley: Occhiobello, Portelogoscuro, the outskirts of Ferrara, Ca' Venier

Premières: Locarno, July 14, 1957; Rome, Nov. 29, 1957; Paris, Dec. 3, 1958; New York, Oct. 22, 1962

Prizes: Critics' Grand Prize, Locarno Festival, 1957; Young Critics' Prize, Cologne Festival, 1957

Aldo has lived for ten years with Irma, whose husband has gone to Australia. Irma, who is no longer in love with Aldo, hears of her husband's death and decides to make a new life for herself with another man. She announces this decision to her lover. Aldo tries to keep her, then ends by beating her in front of the assembled village.

With his love shattered, he sets off along the highway, abandoning his job, and taking with him his daughter by Irma, Rosina. He intends to make a new life for himself with another woman and has a number of adventures, but still pursued by the memory of Irma, he finally returns to the village. There he sees Irma happy, with a new child. Aldo climbs the tower of the refinery where he once worked. As Irma rushes up to the tower after him, he tumbles into the empty air.

L'AVVENTURA (1959-1960)

Story: Michelangelo Antonioni

Screenplay: Michelangelo Antonioni, Elio Bartolini, Tonino
 Guerra
Photography: Aldo Scavarda
Sets: Piero Polletto
Costumes: Adriana Berselli
Music: Giovanni Fusco
Actors: Gabriele Ferzetti, Monica Vitti, Lea Massari, Domi-
 nique Blanchar, Renzo Ricci, James Addams, Dorothy de
 Poliolo, Lelio Luttazzi, Giovanni Petrucci, Esmeralda
 Ruspoli, Enrico Bologna, Franco Cimino, Giovanni
 Danesi, Rita Mole, Renato Pinciroli, Angela Tommasi di
 Lampedusa, Vincenzo Tranchina
Production: A Cino Del Duca Co-Production: Produzioni
 Cinematografiche Europee (Rome) and Société Cinéma-
 tographique Lyre (Paris)
U.S. distributor: Janus Films
Shooting: Rome, Sicily (Lipari Island, Milazzo, Catania,
 Taormina)
Premières: Bologna, Sept. 25, 1960; Milan, Oct. 18, 1960;
 Rome, Nov. 2, 1960; Paris, Sept. 13, 1960; New York,
 April 4, 1961
Prizes: Special Jury Prize and Prix des Ecrivains de Cinéma
 et de Télévision, Cannes Festival, 1960; The British Film
 Institute's Sutherland Trophy, 1960; The Nastro d'ar-
 gento, 1961 (for Giovanni Fusco's music); The Foreign
 Press Prize (for Monica Vitti's performance); Caveja
 d'oro (for the film and for Monica Vitti's performance);
 Saraceno d'oro (for the film and for Monica Vitti's and
 Gabriele Ferzetti's performances); Crystal Star (for
 Monica Vitti's performance)

During a cruise among the Lipari Islands, Anna, a pas-
senger on an elegant yacht, disappears. Her lover, Sandro,
searches for her with the help of Claudia, a friend of Anna's,
and the other guests. Anna's father and the police are
alerted, but the search brings no result.

Sandro is seized with a sudden passion for Claudia. She
tries vainly to resist the same feelings in herself. With the
apparent pretext of continuing the search, the two young
people come together and surrender to their desire. They
live for a few days in perfect happiness at Noto, then at
Taormina. But one evening, when he is at loose ends and
Claudia has decided to stay in her room, Sandro indulges in
a sordid adventure with a hotel call girl. Claudia finds them
together and flees, heartbroken. On the terrace where he
later finds her, Sandro weeps with self-disgust.

In the rising dawn, Claudia sketches a gesture of pardon.

LA NOTTE (1960)

Scenario: Michelangelo Antonioni, Ennio Flaiano, Tonino Guerra

Photography: Gianni di Venanzo

Sets: Piero Zuffi

Music: Giorgio Gaslini

Actors: Jeanne Moreau, Marcello Mastroianni, Monica Vitti, Bernhard Wicki

Production: Emmanuel Cassuto, for Nepi-Film (Rome), Silva-Film (Rome) and Sofitedip (Paris)

U.S. distributor: Lopert Pictures Corp.

Shooting: Milan

Premières: Milan, Jan. 24, 1961; Rome, Feb. 1, 1961; Paris, Feb. 24, 1961; New York, Feb. 19, 1962

Prizes: Golden Bear (Grand Prize), Berlin Festival, 1961; International Cinematographic Press Federation (FI-PRESCI) Prize at the same festival (for the whole body of Antonioni's work to date)

Lidia and Giovanni have been married for ten years. On the day the film takes place, they pay a visit to their friend Tommaso, who is dying in a Milanese hospital. They then attend a cocktail party given to celebrate the publication of Giovanni's new book. But Lidia flees this worldly spectacle and wanders through the suburbs of Milan where she first experienced a love of which she feels quite certain there no longer remains anything but memories.

The evening continues in an expensive night club, then at a party given by a rich industrialist on the grounds of his villa. There Giovanni meets Valentina, his host's daughter; Lidia allows herself to dally for a moment with an elegant idler. The end of the night brings the couple back together. They leave the absurd, pathetic party. Tommaso has died. They have become conscious that their love has disappeared. They embrace in the dawn, but without any certainty of renewed love.

L'ECLISSE (1961)

Story and Screenplay: Michelangelo Antonioni and Tonino Guerra, with collaboration on the screenplay by Elio Bartolini and Ottiero Ottieri

Photography: Gianni di Venanzo

Sets: Piero Polletto.

Music: Giovanni Fusco

Actors: Alain Delon, Monica Vitti, Francisco Rabal, Louis Seigner, Lilla Brignone, Rossana Rory, Mirella Ricciardi

Produced by Robert and Raymond Hakim
U.S. distributor: Times Film Corp.
Shooting: Rome, Verona
Premières: Milan, April 15, 1962; Paris, Oct. 28, 1962; New
York, Dec. 20, 1962

A brief encounter between a man and woman from different environments and with widely diverging problems. Vittoria has just broken off a previous relationship with a man about whom we learn nothing. From this obviously painful experience, she plunges into a happy-go-lucky affair with a young man whose passion is money. Piero makes his living working frantically at the Stock Exchange, where fortunes expand and collapse in a matter of minutes. The relationship between Vittoria and Piero slowly becomes clouded over, and they grow apart almost invisibly. They fail to keep an appointment with each other; at the same time, an eclipse falls over the city, the darkness suggesting both their private emotional desolation and the condition of all human society today.

Bibliography

I. SELECTED ENGLISH BIBLIOGRAPHY

Writings and Statements by Antonioni

"Making a Film Is My Way of Life." *Film Culture* (Spring 1962).
"A Talk with Michelangelo Antonioni on His Work." *Film Culture* (Spring 1962). This is a translation of the transcript of the seminar at the Experimental Film Center in Rome which was published in *Bianco e Nero* and which is quoted from frequently throughout this book.
Screenplays, translated by Louis Brigante. New York, Orion Press, 1963. Contains the scenarios for *Il Grido, L'Avventura, La Notte, L'Eclisse.*
"Eclipse." *Theatre Arts* (July 1962). Brief statement on his concept of the film, with an accompanying one by Monica Vitti. Plus stills.

Studies, Articles, Interviews, Reviews

Alpert, Hollis, "A Talk with Antonioni." *Saturday Review* (October 27, 1962).
Arbasino, Alberto, "Alien Corn." *Atlas* (January 1963). Translation of an article originally published in *Il Mondo.* A polemical critique of sociological "errors" in Antonioni's films.
Aristarco, Guido, *"La Notte and L'Avventura." Film Culture* (Spring 1962).
Bennett, Joseph, "The Essence of Being." *The Hudson Review* (Autumn 1961). Discussion of Antonioni centered on *L'Avventura.*
Cameron, Ian, "Michelangelo Antonioni." *Film Quarterly,* entire issue (Fall 1962). Also published as a pamphlet by Movie Magazine, Ltd., London, 1963.
Clay, Jean, "Michelangelo Antonioni: A Great Master of the Italian Renaissance." *Réalités,* English edition (June 1962).
Doniol-Valcroze, Jacques, "The Rh Factor and the New Cinema," translated by Rose Kaplin and reprinted with the permission of *Cahiers du Cinéma. New York Film Bulletin,* No. 31 (March 27, 1961).

Gilman, Richard, "About Nothing—with Precision." *Theatre Arts* (July 1962). An article about several film-makers and playwrights, with emphasis on Antonioni.

Huston, Penelope, "*L'Avventura*." *Sight and Sound* (Winter 1960-61).

Kauffmann, Stanley, "Arrival of an Artist." *The New Republic* (April 10, 1961).

Labarthe, André-S., "An Interview with Antonioni." *New York Film Bulletin*, No. 34 (May 29, 1961). This is a translation of the interview which appeared in *Cahiers du Cinéma*, No. 112, October 1960.

———, Filmography of Antonioni. *New York Film Bulletin*, Series Two, No. 9 (35) (June 12, 1961). Translation of the filmography which appeared in *Cahiers du Cinéma*, No. 112 (October 1960); contains information on the documentaries which does not appear in the present volume.

MacDonald, Dwight, "Antonioni Before *L'A.*" *Esquire* (June 1961).

———, "The Grandeur and Misery of Antonioni." *Esquire* (May 1962). General discussion, plus review of *Lu Notte*.

Manceaux, Michèle, "An Interview with Antonioni." *Sight and Sound* (Winter 1960-61). This is the original, fuller text of an interview first printed in *L'Express* on September 8, 1960.

Simon, John, "The Sour Truth About the Sweet Life." *Horizon* (September 1961). About *La Dolce Vita* and *L'Avventura*.

Strick, Philip, *Antonioni*. London, Motion Publications, 1963. An extensive monograph, with a brief introduction by Antonioni.

Young, Vernon, "Of Night, Fire and Water." *The Hudson Review* (Summer 1962). Discussion of *La Notte* (and Buñuel's *Viridiana*).

II. ITALIAN BIBLIOGRAPHY (*in chronological order within sections*)

Principal Writings by Antonioni

PUBLISHED IN *Cinema:*

"La Scuola delle Moglie" (February 25, 1940).

"Allarmi Inutili" (April 10, 1940).

"Inaugurazione" (September 10, 1940).

"La Sorpresa Venezia" (October 10, 1940).

"Due Lustri di Sonoro," in collaboration with Gianni Puccini (December 25, 1940).

"Per una Storia della Mostra" (September 10 and 25, 1941).

"Suggerimenti di Hegel (December 10, 1942).

"L'Herbier sulle Orme di Méliès" (January 25, 1943).

"Battere le Mani" (May 1, 1943).

"La Pazienza del Cinema" (January 30, 1949).

"Brevario del Cinema" (Nos. 11, 16, 20, 37 and 41, 1949).
PUBLISHED IN *Lo Schermo:*
"Prévert e Carné" (August-September, 1943).
PUBLISHED IN *Primata:*
"Commento a un'Emigrazione" (May 15, 1943).
PUBLISHED IN *Cosmopolità:*
"Miseria e Poesia di Charlot" (in "Charlie Chaplin," pp. 22-24).
PUBLISHED IN *Film d'Oggi:*
"Film di Tutto il Mondo a Roma" (October 6 and 10, November 3, 1945).
PUBLISHED IN *Fiera Letteraria:*
"Marcel Carné, Avvero Quasi un Ritratto" (May 30, 1946).
PUBLISHED IN *Film Rivista:*
"Frigida America" (August 31, 1946).
"Omaggio a Clair" (September 13, 1946).
"Omaggio a Renoir" (September 19, 1946).
PUBLISHED IN *Bianco e Nero:*
"Marcel Carné, Parigino" (October, 1948).
"Lettera a Michele Lacalàmita" (May, 1958).
"Colloquo con Michelangelo Antonioni" (June, 1958). Seminar with students at the Experimental Film Center, Rome.
"Crisi e Neorealismo, Risposta al Questionario di *Bianco e Nero*" (September, 1958).
PUBLISHED IN *Cinema Nuovo:*
"Un Passo Avanti" (March 1, 1953).
"Stanotte Hanno Sparato" (April 15, 1953).
"Antonioni Risponde a Chiarini" (May 15, 1953).
"Annuale e biennale?" (August 15, 1953).
"Suicidi in Città" (March 15, 1954).
"Domande e Rispote" (January 25, 1955).
"Domande e Rispote" (April 25, 1955).
"Fare un Film e per Me Vivere" (March-April, 1959).
PUBLISHED IN *Successo* (Milan):
"Ho una Storia Vera Che Non Posso Girare" (February, 1961).

Books and Pamphlets

Il Grido. The screenplay, presented by Elio Bartolini. Bologna, Cappelli, 1957. This was the first Antonioni screenplay to be presented in Cappelli's excellent series entitled "Dal Soggetto al Film," edited by Renzo Renzi.
Tino Ranieri, *Michelangelo Antonioni* (Lectures given at the Centro Universitario Cinematogràfico of the University of Trieste), 1957-58.
Fabio Carpi, *Michelangelo Antonioni.* Parma, Guandi, 1958.

———, *Cinema italiano del Dopoguerra*. Milan, Scharz, 1958.
Bruno Voglino, *Michelangelo Antonioni*. *Centrofilm*, No. 3, Centro Universitario Cinematogràfico, Turin, 1959.
Various authors: *Michelangelo Antonioni*. Centro Universitario Cinematogràfico, Milan, 1960.
L'Avventura di Michelangelo Antonioni. The screenplay, with the story of its production, presented by Tommaso Chiaretti. Bologna, Cappelli, 1960. No. 15 in the series "Dal Soggetto al Film."
L'Eclisse. The screenplay, presented by John Francis Lane. Bologna, Cappelli, 1962. Includes sequences in the script later deleted, plus articles by various contributors. No. 23 in the series "Dal Soggetto al Film."

Interviews and Statements

G. Guidi and L. Malerba, "What Do You Think of the Public?" (Italian title unavailable) *Cinema* (November 1, 1951).
G. Calderoni, "What Is Your Opinion of Censorship?" (Italian title unavailable) *Cinema* (March 15, 1952).
"Antonioni Recalls the Beginnings of His Career." (Italian title unavailable) *Gazzetta Padana* (October 17, 1960).

Articles

Guido Bezzola, "Renoir, Visconti, Antonioni." *Cinema Nuovo* (September 1, 1953).
Giuseppe Sibilla, "M. Antonioni." *Bianco e Nero* (January, 1954).
Renzo Renzi, "Stile e Coscienza Morale di M.A." *Emilia* (April, 1954).
Francesco Bolzoni, "Un Ritratto di Antonioni." *Revista del Cinema Italiano* (October, 1954).
Nedo Ivaldi, "Antonioni e l'Educazione Visiva." *Filmcritica* (November–December, 1955).
Fernalda di Giammateo, "M. Antonioni," *Communità* (Milan), February, 1956).
Francesco Bolzoni, "Un regista: M. Antonioni." *Ferrania* (Milan), (February, 1957).
Fabio Carpi, "M. Antonioni," *Cinema Nuovo*, No. 103 (Milan), (March 15, 1957).
Giuseppe Ferrara, *Il Nuovo Cinema Italiano*. Florence, Le Monnier, 1957, pp. 268-271 and 322-329.
Enrico Roda, "37 Domande a M.A." *Tempo* (July 4, 1957).
Giambattista Cavallero, "M. Antonioni, Simbolo di una Generazione"; "Filmografia"; "Antonioni e la Critica, Bibliografia a Eura di Giuseppe Ferrara." *Bianco e Nero* (September 1957).
L.-G. Gerardo Colombo, "Coerenza Estetica e Morale nell' Opera di Antonioni." *Il Cittadino* (February 8, 1959).

G. Tumiati, "Antonioni uno e due," *L'Illustrazione italiana* (September, 1960).

G.-C. Castello, "Coerenza di Antonioni." *Il Punto* (October 8, 1960).

G. Mazzocchi, "Le Cinque Strade di Antonioni." *Il Punto* (March 11, 1961).

III. FRENCH BIBLIOGRAPHY (*in chronological order within sections*)

Writings by Antonioni

"Un Scène Inédite du *Cri*," translated and presented by P.-L. Thirard. *Les Lettres Françaises* (December 4, 1958).

"Une Journée" (written in 1942). *Positif*, No. 30 (July 1959).

"*La Terre Tremble* de Visconti." Critical article originally published in *Bianco e Nero*, 1949. Translated by André Bouissy. *Cinéma 59*, No. 38 (July 1959).

"Pourquoi J'Ai Fait *L'Avventura*." A statement distributed at Cannes when the film was first presented there. *Les Lettres Françaises* (May 26, 1960) and *Cinéma 60*, No. 50 (October 1960).

"Mon Film (*La Notte*). *L'Humanité-Dimanche* (February 26, 1961).

Books and Pamphlets

Premier Plan, No. 15. Contains a critical biography by P.-L. Thirard and, in translation, Antonioni's scenario for *The Gay Girls of 1924* (first published in *Cinema Nuovo*, No. 38); excerpts from other screenplays; and additional writings by Antonioni. Lyons, Serdoc, 1961.

"*L'Avventura*" *de Michelangelo Antonioni*. French edition of the book first published in Italy by Cappelli. Translated by Michèle Causse. Paris, Buchet-Chastel, 1961. Excerpts from the Cappelli book, translated by others, were published in *Premier Plan*, No. 15, and *Cahiers du Cinéma* (both August 1960).

La Nuit. The screenplay of *La Notte*, translated by Michèle Causse. Paris, Buchet-Chastel, 1961.

Interviews and Statements

André Bazin, Michel Mayoux and Jean-José Richer, "Interviews et Entretiens du Festival." *Cahiers du Cinéma*, No. 27 (October 1953).

Partial translation of Antonioni's "Colloque avec les Élèves du Centre Expérimental de Rome" (first published in *Bianco e Nero*, June 1958) plus a bio-filmography. *Cinéma 58*, No. 30 (September-October 1958).

"Questions à Antonioni." *Positif*, No. 30 (July 1959). Replies to an inquiry conducted by the French National Radio in connection with the Université Radiophonique Internationale.

"Le Livre Blanc du Cinéma," *La Table Ronde,* No. 149 (May 1960).

Georges Sadoul, "Michelangelo Antonioni tel que je l'ai vu." *Les Lettres Françaises* (May 26, 1960).

Michèle Manceaux, "Entretien avec Michelangelo Antonioni." *L'Express* (September 8, 1960).

Nicole Zand and Louise Marcorelles, "Antonioni et le Monde des Sentiments." *France-Observateur* (September 15, 1960).

François Maurin, "'En Tournant *L'Avventura* J'ai Vécu Cinq Mois Épuisants, mais Extraordinaires.'" *L'Humanité-Dimanche* (September 25, 1960).

André-S. Labarthe, "Entretien avec Michelangelo Antonioni," followed by a bio-filmography translated from the Italian by M. Parolini and Jeanne Imhauser. *Cahiers du Cinéma,* No. 112 (October 1960).

André-S. Labarthe, "Quatre Questions à Antonioni." *France-Observateur* (February 23, 1961).

Sylvain Roumette, "Au bout de *La Nuit.*" A conversation with Antonioni. *Clarté,* No. 34.

Michel Butor, "Rencontre avec Antonioni." *Les Lettres Françaises,* No. 880 (June 1961).

Oriana Fallaci, "Visite à Antonioni." *Positif,* No. 44 (March 1962).

Articles

J. Doniol-Valcroze, "La Photo du Mois." *Cahiers du Cinéma,* No. 70 (April 1957).

Pierre Billard, "M. Antonioni: Un Cinéaste du 'Mal de Vivre.'" *France-Observateur* (December 4, 1958).

Henri Agel, "Michelangelo Antonioni," in his book *Les Grands Cinéastes.* Paris, Éditions Universitaires, 1959, pp. 273-277.

René Gilson, "Michelangelo Antonioni de *Gente del Po* à *Il Grido.*" *Les Temps Modernes,* No. 158 (April 1959).

G. Viazzi and P.-L. Thirard, "Un Écrivain Nommé Antonioni." *Positif,* No. 30 (July 1959).

André-S. Labarthe, "Antonioni Hier et Demain." *Cahiers du Cinéma,* No. 110 (August 1960).

Jean Collet, "Antonioni ou le Desert de l'Amour." *Radio-Cinéma,* No. 559 (October 2, 1960).

"Cinémonde Fait le Procès de M. Antonioni." *Cinémonde* (January 31,

"Qui Êtes-Vous, Michelangelo Antonioni?" *Cité Panorama,* Lyons (January-February 1961).

Jean de Bongnie, "Michelangelo Antonioni, Signe de Contradiction." *Amis du Film et de la TV,* No. 66 (April 1961).

"Découverte d'Antonioni." *Télérama,* No. 585 (April 1961).

Jean-Louis Curtis, "Antonioni au Naturel." *Combat* (April 20, 1961).

René Gilson, "Antonioni, une Question Inquiète." *Cinéma 61*, No. 56 (May 1961).

Roger Tailleur, "Vive *La Nuit.*" *Positif*, No. 39 (May 1961).

Jean Wagner, "La Nuit N'Est Pas Tendre." *Cahiers du Cinéma*, No. 119 (May 1961).

"Les Magistrales Leçons d'Antonioni." *Cinéma Chez Soi*, No. 34 (May 1961).

Pierre Marcabru, "Antonioni: La Poésie et le Désenchantement." *Arts* (June 14, 1961).

Roger Boussinot, "*L'Eclipse.*" *Arts*, No. 880 (September 1962).

Michel Mardore, "Antonioni, Je Suis un Incurable Optimiste." *Les Lettres Françaises*, No. 942 (September 1962).

Robert Benayoun, "*L'Eclipse*, le Regne de l'Object." *France-Observateur*, No. 644 (September 1962).

André-S: Labarthe, "Promethée Enchaîné" (*L'Eclisse*). *Cahiers du Cinéma*, No. 136 (October 1962).

Alberto Arbasino, "Antonioni, la Culture et le Metteur en Scène." *France-Observateur*, No. 649 (October 1962).

"*L'Eclipse.*" *Image et Son*, No. 152 (June 1962).

"Antonioni Expliqué par les Philosophes." *Cinéma 62*, No. 70 (November 1962).

Notes on Part I

1. EARLY LIFE AND THE DOCUMENTARIES:

1. From "Fare un Film e per Me Vivere," *Cinema Nuovo*, March-April 1959. Complete text published in *Film Culture*, Spring 1962.
2. "Entretien avec Michelangelo Antonioni," *Cahiers du Cinéma*, No. 112, October 1960.
3. A transcript of this seminar was published in *Bianco e Nero*, the monthly publication of the Experimental Film Center in Rome.
4. Some of these were published in French translation in *Premier Plan*, No. 15, and in *Positif*, No. 30, July 1959.
5. Excerpt from "Fare un Film e per Me Vivere."
6. Excerpt from text in *Il Corriere Padano*, February 18, 1939.
7. The world situation was soon to halt all preparations for the exposition, which was supposed to have opened in 1942.
8. From "Le Cinéma pendant la Guerre," in *Histoire Générale du Cinéma* by Georges Sadoul.
9. In his book *Il Cinema Italiano*, Carlo Lizzani gives a splendid account of the process that lay behind this fermentation.
10. This was a film set in fifteenth-century Venice.
11. Antonioni discusses these same recollections in his seminar with the students at the Experimental Center, published in *Bianco e Nero*.
12. On this point, see Antonioni's "Une Journée" in *Positif*, No. 30, July 1959.
13. G. R. Aldo (his real name, and the one listed in some Italian film-ographies, was Aldo Graziani) was at that time one of the best cameramen in Paris. It was Antonioni who introduced him to Visconti in about 1946, thus enabling him to become chief cameraman for *La Terra Trema*. Aldo was killed in an automobile accident a few years later.
14. *Positif*, No. 30, July 1959.

2. THE FIRST FEATURES:

1. *L'Express,* September 8, 1960.
2. *La Table Ronde,* No. 149, May 1960.
3. *Positif,* No. 30, July 1959.
4. *Cahiers du Cinéma,* No. 37.
5. Michel Mayoux, in *Cahiers du Cinéma,* No. 5, September 1951.
6. Statement made to Yvonne Baby, in *Le Monde,* September 16, 1960.
7. *Cinéma 53,* Édit. du Cerf, 1954.
8. Seminar at the Experimental Center, published in *Bianco e Nero.*
9. *Chroniques de Cinéma et de Télévision,* No. 7, quoted by P.-L. Thirard in *Premier Plan,* No. 15.
10. From "Suicidi in Città," by Antonioni, in *Cinema Nuovo,* March 15, 1954.
11. Robert Benayoun in *Positif,* No. 30.
12. Marcel Martin in *Cinéma 60,* No. 51.

3. LE AMICHE:

1. *Radio-Cinéma,* No. 142, October 5, 1952.
2. *Cinéma 58,* No. 30.
3. Quoted by Georges Sadoul in *Les Lettres Françaises,* September 22, 1960.
4. Quoted in *Cahiers du Cinéma,* No. 112.
5. Seminar at the Experimental Center, published in *Bianco e Nero.*

4. IL GRIDO:

1. *Radio-Cinéma,* December 21, 1958.
2. *Cahiers du Cinéma,* No. 112, October 1960.
3. On this point, P.-L. Thirard writes very tellingly in *Premier Plan,* No. 15: "In what is nothing more than a secondary episode, Antonioni abruptly unbalances the world, brings us to the edge of the abyss."
4. "*Le Cri,* ou la Faillité de Nos Sentiments," *Positif,* No. 35.

5. L'AVVENTURA:

1. Remark quoted by Georges Sadoul in *Les Lettres Françaises,* May 26, 1960.
2. Both quoted passages in this paragraph from the seminar at the Experimental Center, published in *Bianco e Nero.*
3. With Michèle Manceaux, in *L'Express,* September 8, 1960.
4. Interview with Georges Sadoul in *Les Lettres Françaises,* May 26, 1960.

6. LA NOTTE AND THE FUTURE:

1. *Le Figaro Littéraire,* February 25, 1961.
2. Seminar at the Experimental Center, published in *Bianco e Nero.*
3. Reported by Richard Gilman in "About Nothing—with Precision," *Theatre Arts,* July 1962.

About the Author

PIERRE LEPROHON is a French film critic who has published ten books in his field, including works on Charles Chaplin, the German cinema, and the history of French films. From 1950 to 1958, he was chief editor of Unifrance Film. Since 1930, he has lived in Paris.

About the Translator

SCOTT SULLIVAN was graduated from Yale in 1958 and afterward studied at Cambridge for two years. He then lived in Paris, writing, for two years; during that time, his first novel—*The Shortest Gladdest Years*—was published (Simon and Schuster, 1962).

R.C. (B)

Mass Mus.

PRINTED IN U.S.A.

GAYLORD